W9-BGA-664

PRAISE FOR ONE TEAM, ONE SPIRIT: INSPIRATION FOR THE CHRISTIAN COACH

Dr. Jim Pingel has gone off for a triple-double in this great work: *One Team, One Spirit*! Faithfulness. Authenticity. Practicality. It is truly authentic! I arrived on the campus of Concordia University Wisconsin at the same time as Jim. As a student serving as Sports Information Director, I saw his determination and faithfulness firsthand. As a parent of a student who was educated in a school administrated by him, I saw him live this out authentically. As a pastor and coach who led teams that played against Jim's son, I love the practicality of this book. I wish I would have had it in my library back then! What I love most about it is that it debunks the great myth of "ball is life." Dr. Pingel makes it clear that life is only in Jesus Christ!

The format of this devotional book is tremendous! A coach can't give away what he or she doesn't have. For the devotions to be first for the coach, then for the players, captures the beauty of what it means to be Christian and coach at the same time. The Christian receives and then gives glory to God by serving others. A coach who uses this book as a model will show this clearly! Coach receives and then gives. The Lord is praised, and the players are blessed! Thanks to Jim for this great work! And to God be the glory! In Christ is the victory!

Rev. Dr. Nathan Meador
Senior Pastor and former basketball coach,
St. John Lutheran Church and School, Plymouth, WI
Assistant Coordinator for Stewardship, LCMS Office of National Mission

This book is an excellent resource for coaches who want to reach athletes beyond the *x*'s and *o*'s. Jim presents a game plan for coaches to use with their teams and with their own spiritual preparation for coaching. Having a plan for the spiritual growth of our athletes is critical to having an eternal impact. I would recommend this book for coaches of all levels.

Micah Parker, PhD
Director of Athletics, California Baptist University

Coach Jim Pingel provides an excellent resource and reminder for all coaches who desire to use the platform of athletics for the purpose of more than wins. This is a must for a first-year coach and I believe could become an annual part of veteran coaches' preparation and reflection to best serve their teams. While professing to not being much of a shooter or defender, with compliments including "you reverse the ball well" and "you are the best of the top 5 worst players I have coached," Pingel hits a 3 at the buzzer for the win with his book.

Chris Hahn
Headmaster, Prince of Peace Christian School
Little League and Middle School coach

Sports provide innumerable teachable moments. In *One Team, One Spirit*, Jim Pingel has created an inspiring resource for Christian coaches, athletes, and leaders. The book meshes faith and sports to provide a valuable tool for coaches, regardless of where they are in their personal faith walks. Dr. Pingel incorporates lively stories from his years as athlete, coach, administrator, father, and fan into forty-five devotions organized around the annual sports calendar. An easy, user-friendly read in bite-size pieces. Enjoy it yourself and give it to your coaches!

Dr. David Hahn
Executive Director, Association of Lutheran Secondary Schools
Head of School Emeritus, Long Island Lutheran Schools

Dr. Pingel's devotional text is the perfect tool for both rookie and established coaches who are looking to purposefully integrate the faith into their coaching. The unique structure of the text gives coaches the opportunity to reflect before presenting devotions to the team, resulting in deeper understanding for both coaches and players. Straightforward, honest, and rooted firmly in Scripture, Pingel's devotions meet coaches and players where they are at, regardless of sport, season, or record. I strongly recommend this book for any Christian athletic program.

Mrs. Jenna Roeske
Sheboygan Lutheran High School
English Department Chair
Varsity Dance Team Coach

This will be an excellent resource for coaches who would like to incorporate Christian growth for their team into their coaching plans. Jim has always looked for ways to help his athletes become stronger in their faith in Jesus. He has a knack of seeing spiritual lessons in the daily ups and downs every coach and team experience.

David Lane
Teacher, Coach, and Director of Servant Life at Mayer Lutheran H. S.
36 years at MLHS, 5 at East Monona Community School—Moorhead, IA
Member of the Minnesota Baseball Coaches
Hall of Fame—Class of 2016

One Team, One Spirit is an outstanding read, useful for coaches of all levels. The author's presentation of a devotional topic is not only appropriate for coaches but also equips a coach with the necessary tools to lead a devotion, regardless of a coach's religious background. The author's concept of two scoreboards is an especially powerful message to coaches, parents, student-athletes, and administrators.

Shawn Cassidy
Men's Basketball Coach
Concordia University Wisconsin

The relationship between coaches and their athletes can be life-changing. Coaches would like to think they impact athletes in a positive manner and help train them for a positive earthly life. Jim has written a book that will impact coaches and athletes in their earthly life, but more important, it provides a guide for eternal life. The lessons go beyond what impact they could have on a team; they show how a team can be a witness to the world. All coaches can use the examples in this book to create that special relationship with their athletes that extends beyond the court or field. This book would be a valuable asset to any coach's library. It is exciting to see someone put together a guide to help Christian coaches fulfill God's calling. Everyone who has known Jim knows he lives his life being a role model to the people around him. Jim has put together this book in a way that describes his life. This book is genuine and impactful to all Christians.

Pete Gnan
Director of Athletics
Concordia University Chicago

Each chapter challenges you to think about who you are as a Christian coach, player, parent, or fan, and the message that you want to portray to everyone associated with your program. I thoroughly enjoyed the transition from fall, winter, and spring sports and how each chapter included a devotion or prayer focused on faith development. Whether you're a coach, player, parent, or fan, this book helps to reinforce "What Did Jesus Do" by providing suggestions aimed towards the spiritual development of Christian leaders on and off the court.

Coach Mike Scheele
Head Coach, Girls Varsity Basketball
Sheboygan Lutheran High School

Jim Pingel's *One Team, One Spirit: Inspiration for the Christian Coach* is the ideal book for one who sees coaching as a ministry. He masterfully connects sports analogies with the Christian life in clever, precise devotions which will challenge the coach and enlighten the players who use it. His background as student, parent, coach, and administrator in Christian schools gives him a unique perspective from which to reflect.

Coach Randy Rogers
Head Men's Basketball Coach
Concordia University Chicago

There have been countless books written about coaching skills and the importance of athletics in shaping people's lives, as well as books on Christian faith and living. What Jim Pingel has done is combine them into a resource for Christian coaches, especially those looking to make Christ the center of their team culture. Through self-deprecating wit and a clear mission-driven narrative, Pingel has designed a practical guide to bringing faith to the front and center of every practice, game, and team event. Particularly useful are the devotions and prayers to be used by teams from grade school through college to practice and play to Christ's glory, not our own. I strongly recommend this work to those who are just breaking into coaching, or have been doing it for decades. If one truly believes team culture supersedes game-day strategy, then this book will help you achieve your goals.

Patrick W. Steele, PhD
Associate Professor of History
Assistant Softball Coach, Concordia University Wisconsin

Competitive sports programs for school-aged student athletes connect kids, parents, and coaches in an evocative and dynamic environment. Often what is evoked, however, seems far removed from the idea of fun and physical fitness, much less the ideal of character building, and life-lesson forming potential of athletics. In our culture, the elusive pursuit of athletic prowess often fuels aspirations of young athletes, their moms and dads, and their coaches in unhelpful and unhealthy ways. It does not have to be that way.

Perspective matters. For Christians, the Bible informs our perspectives on sportsmanship and fair play; discipline and dedication; team-building and goal-setting; and using the gifts God gives us to His glory. Jim Pingel loves sports. He also loves kids. Above all, he loves Jesus. As a former coach, a Christian educator, and a parent of kids who were a part of school teams, Dr. Pingel recognizes the value of competitive athletics in helping young people grow in mind, body, and spirit. This thoughtful devotional, replete with biblical insight and reference, will become an indispensable resource for Christian coaches eager to help their teams and athletes to enjoy their sport—and their lives—from the winsome perspective of faith in Christ.

Dr. Patrick T. Ferry, MDiv
President, Concordia University Wisconsin and
Concordia University Ann Arbor

ONE TEAM ONE SPIRIT

INSPIRATION *for the*
CHRISTIAN COACH

JIM PINGEL

CONCORDIA PUBLISHING HOUSE • SAINT LOUIS

Dedicated to my two favorite student-athletes of all time—
my son, Josh, and my daughter, Josie.
May you both always keep the crown of life
God has awarded you.

Concordia
Publishing House

Published by Concordia Publishing House
3558 S. Jefferson Ave., St. Louis, MO 63118-3968
1-800-325-3040 • cph.org

Manufactured in the United States of America

Library of Congress Cataloging-in-Publication Data

Names: Pingel, Jim, author.

Title: One team, one spirit : inspiration for the Christian coach / Jim Pingel.

Description: St. Louis : Concordia Publishing House, 2017.

Identifiers: LCCN 2017019862 (print) I LCCN 2017028887 (ebook) I ISBN

9780758659491 I ISBN 9780758659484

Subjects: LCSH: Athletes--Religious life. I Coaching (Athletics)--Religious

aspects--Christianity.

Classification: LCC BV4596.A8 (ebook) I LCC BV4596.A8 P56 2017 (print) I DDC

248.8/8--dc23

LC record available at https://lccn.loc.gov/2017019862

1 2 3 4 5 6 7 8 9 10   26 25 24 23 22 21 20 19 18 17

TABLE  OF CONTENTS

WINTER

SPRING

THE CAN-DO LIST

FOREWORD

I've always been thankful for the wonderful gift God has given us in the game of basketball. Whether watching, playing, cheering, practicing, or coaching, basketball is a game enjoyed by millions. I have been truly blessed to be able to play hoops, coach it, and experience some of the greatest moments in my life because of this game.

When I was just starting my teaching career, I was given the opportunity to coach at the middle school level. I immediately fell in love with coaching. Spending time with the players, building relationships, learning and growing, teaching and competing, sharing the wins and the losses—everything about it was exciting to me. I moved on to the high school level and was an assistant for a number of years under Coach Tom Desotell, one of the most respected and successful coaches in the history of Wisconsin high school basketball. When God gave me the opportunity to be the varsity coach at Sheboygan Area Lutheran High School, I was able to build a basketball program where Christ was at the center. Believe me, I learned more from my experience there than I taught and am so thankful for all of the players, assistants, staff, and fans who were there with me to support me throughout seventeen seasons.

During this basketball ride, I have had the best assistant coach a guy could have in my wife, Carol. She has been the backbone of our family and invaluable to my success as a coach. We are blessed with three wonderful children, John, Hannah, and Sam, all who participated in sports that provided us with lots of memories. It was an awesome opportunity for me to be John and Sam's coach for all four years of high school, where they both had many successes. Topping it off was Sam's senior year, when we experienced an incredible comeback to win the Boys Division 5 State Tournament Championship in 2012. I didn't think it could get any better than that, but then we were blessed to be a part of the most historic seasons of Wisconsin basketball during Sam's time as a

Badger—winning two Big 10 Tournament titles, taking two trips to the Final Four, and making it to the championship game against Duke. The night our family sat together at the 2015 NBA Draft and I heard my son's name called as he was selected by the Houston Rockets in the first round was an incredibly proud moment for me. Glory to God!

Throughout these experiences, I believe our faith has helped us to stay grounded and to keep everything in perspective. God says He has a plan for us and for our future, and believing and trusting in His plan has helped our family through all the good and bad times. I know as a husband, father, coach, and teacher, relying on God to have it all under control has helped me each and every step of the way. Being able to lean on my faith and family has made coaching so much easier and so much more fun!

Jim Pingel was the Executive Director at Sheboygan Area Lutheran High during my coaching years and while our kids were students there. The school flourished under his guidance and leadership, and I was grateful for his support of our basketball program. As a coach himself, he was a good sounding board with words of wisdom when needed. Because Jim would never toot his own horn, I honestly didn't realize what a successful coach he had been until I read this book. To be selected as High School Coach of the Year in Minnesota is quite an honor and a huge accomplishment! But more important is that he focused on Christ as the head of his program. The girls he coached not only improved on the court, but they were better Christian leaders because of Coach Pingel's guidance. His leadership, hard work, and dedication rubbed off on his players. Jim's trust in his Savior is evident in all that he does.

That trust is the key principal of this book, *One Team, One Spirit: Inspiration for the Christian Coach*. What a great idea to have a book like this to serve as a devotional guide to assist coaches throughout an entire season. Not only is it a great resource for sharing the Gospel with the players, it's also a helpful tool for coaches to grow in their faith. While I was reading it, I kept thinking how I wish I had this when I started at Lutheran High. Coming from a public school setting, I wasn't always comfortable leading a prayer or reading a devotion because I had never done it before. I'm sure I stumbled many times, and this book would have been such a big help to me! A great deal of thought, prayer, time, and effort was put into this coach's manual. I recommend it for every coach of any sport as a spiritual guide for preparing for meetings, practices, and games. The Christian lessons that we can give to our players are of utmost importance. These are the lessons that will stick with the student athletes for the rest of their lives, and that they, in turn, will pass on to future players of this wonderful gift of the game.

Job well done, Coach Pingel!

Todd Dekker
Father and Former Lutheran High School Basketball Coach

ACKNOWLEDGEMENTS

The first people I want to thank are the boys and girls, men and women, I was privileged and honored to coach over the years. Many of my favorite life memories include those special moments and relationships that only a coach and player can share.

The second group of people I would like to thank are the parents of the players I coached, those who entrusted their sons and daughters to my care for hours each day. Sometimes they disagreed with how I rewarded their child with playing time, but most were warm supporters, friends, and people whom I genuinely enjoyed spending time with even beyond team meals.

I am grateful for those who read my manuscript and provided valuable feedback. Jeff Jurss, a colleague in Christ and an outstanding cross-country coach, is one of my favorite Christian leaders because he intentionally infuses Scripture and faith into his program. His encouragement and enthusiasm for the project were most appreciated.

Dave Pingel, my younger brother and fellow basketball junkie, provided constructive criticism and basketball anecdotes that he knew I would treasure. Competitive brothers are not always good about complimenting or praising each another. When he told me this was one of the best books he had ever read, he made my day.

Having your mother and father edit your manuscript might be a bit unusual in the publishing industry. Yet, Alva Lea, a former English teacher, and Rev. Dr. James Pingel, a professor and retired Lutheran Church—Missouri Synod pastor, spent countless hours reviewing the material and offered invaluable editorial assistance and biblical discernment. Not only did they provide much humor and comic relief as I reviewed their differing opinions on sentence structure and verbiage, but they also warmed my heart with the time they took to discuss the implications of the work. They are the best coaches I ever had.

Finally, I want to thank my wife, Michelle, who never complained during all those years when I came home late, stayed up late watching film, and remained grumpy the next day when my teams did not perform as I desired. She remains the head coach of our family and two wonderful children and is really the co-author of this book in so many ways.

LESSONS LEARNED FROM A BASKETBALL LIFE

Behind every mission is a story—in this case, a basketball story. Thus, before you absorb and meditate on the devotions in *One Team, One Spirit: Inspiration for the Christian Coach*, I want to provide the background, inspiration, and purpose of this work and how I hope it will touch you and make a difference in your life.

While not an epic tale like *Hoosiers*, this book has been in the making for more than four decades. God has blessed me as a player, coach, fan, and father, and He has taught me many life lessons through youth sports, particularly through the game of basketball. I wish I could tell you that I hit the game-winning shot in a state championship game during my high school years or that my kids knocked down a buzzer beater at the end of their state championship games. Alas, neither happened. I also wish I could give an account of how I coached a team to a state championship title. While my team once got close, this goal has gone unrealized. Instead, my basketball story, like those of so many of you reading this work, is both common and unique, singular and multi-faceted, pedestrian and life-changing. Through it all, God has used the game of basketball to shape my Christian worldview and to equip me as His disciple. As Romans 8:28 declares, "And we know that for those who love God all things work together for good, for those who are called according to His purpose." Let me tell you the ways.

A Family Affair

Like many of you, my basketball life began as a youth basketball player in the local recreation league. The coach happened to be my father, a Lutheran Church—Missouri Synod pastor, and I have fond memories of those first days of organized basketball. Dad knew a little bit about match-up zone defenses— he knew a whole lot more about Jesus and Scripture. Nevertheless, we had fun. Even with early elementary school teams, Dad was constantly tinkering with junk defenses, defensive matchups, and scouting opposing third- and fourth-grade teams. Everyone played 2–3 zone defense in those days, so when Dad introduced the 3–2 zone defense, I thought he was as cutting edge as James Naismith and the most ingenious rebel since Martin Luther. Someday, I told myself, I want to coach like my Dad and not be afraid to deploy different defensive systems and approach the game with new ideas. He instilled confidence in me and made the game both fun *and* interesting.

Blessed with great friends at school and in my neighborhood, I constantly played two-on-two and three-on-three basketball in driveways all across Sun Prairie, Wisconsin. The first team to score 100 points won. When one team reached 50, we would take a ten-minute halftime break. We had epic wars and clashes on the concrete and simply loved playing the game. Those neighborhood games truly brought the purest joy, as far as my playing days go, in all my years associated with the game of basketball. Competing and playing hard, especially with people I enjoyed being around, built deep friendships, trust, and a spirit of camaraderie hard to explain to others who have never experienced the delight of teamwork.

Even though I was short and unable to dribble or shoot with any prowess, I participated (I use the term liberally) on public school teams during my middle school years. The only time I got off the bench is when I fell off. Nevertheless, I practiced and competed hard every day. I quickly learned that the only thing you really could control as a player was your hustle and how hard you played on defense.

During my first year of high school, I made the freshman team—the freshman C team, more precisely. Sun Prairie High School had three freshman teams and the C team was, as you might assume by the letter grade, not so talented. I got to play some, but not in real games. Instead, I played during *halftime* of the C team games. We called ourselves the "three-minute crew," for the conference had agreed to the let the bottom five players on each freshman team play for three minutes (running clock) at halftime (with no officials). We huffed and puffed (it was hard to stay in shape when you never played) and hacked anyone (remember there were no officials) who moved in our general vicinity.

During my individual meeting with the coach at the end of my freshman year of basketball, my coach complimented me on my hustle, defensive tenacity, and positive attitude. Gracious and generous in his praise (if not playing time), he even wrote these flattering words of encouragement down on a little index card, which I still possess to this day. I think he really meant every word he said to me. Of course, he *did not* say the program had great and grand plans for me in the future. The coach's kind words aside, I got the sugarcoated message: I was not good enough to play high school basketball. And, truthfully, I knew I was not good enough. Sports have a unique way of humbling and bringing truth and reality to the surface. I attended a large, public high school with physically talented, tall, and strong athletes storming the hallways. With little talent, less height and quickness, and no desire to sit on the bench anymore, I made a decision to quit basketball. I thought my playing days were over.

Early retirement brought some good news: No longer playing high school basketball, I had more time to follow college basketball. I subscribed to three or four basketball periodicals and watched and recorded games on television religiously almost every night. At one time, I had more than one hundred taped college basketball games, and I rewatched parts of these athletic contests almost every night. I loved studying the game. I thought, perhaps, I would coach someday.

The very first book I ever read from cover to cover was John Feinstein's enthralling and engrossing portrait of Bobby Knight in *A Season on the Brink*. Ironically, for a LCMS preacher's kid who rarely cussed and never ever threw a chair across a basketball court, I absolutely revered Bobby Knight for years after reading Feinstein's book. His dedicated principles and earnest faith in his system and program were compelling and resonated with me. Great leaders possess strong convictions, a philosophy, a worldview, a vision, and a strategic plan on how to live and lead.

Leadership and Coaching Mentors

In the fall of 1988, I set foot on the campus of Concordia University Wisconsin (Concordia College at the time) determined to become a high school basketball coach and social studies teacher, in that order. During those first few weeks on campus, I got the harebrained idea that the best way to learn the drills, offensive and defensive sets, motivational tactics, and *how to teach* the game was to learn and play under a college coach and basketball system. Thus, without having played organized, competitive basketball since my freshman C team half-time experience, I showed up on the first day of practice as a short, out-of-shape white guy with no handle, no jump shot, no athleticism, and no clue what it took to play college basketball. If Notre Dame had its Rudy, Concordia had its Jimmy.

Then I had to guard someone. In those first weeks of practice, I recognized my teammates only by their backside. These former high school all-state and all-regional players from around the country, now Concordia Falcons, blew by me, through me, and over me in almost every drill. They were so quick, strong, and athletic that I could not even grab and hold their jerseys to keep up. Looking back, I cringe at how bad I must have looked. My teammates must have thought I was recovering from a severe car accident or disease, anything, because no one this short and un-athletic would ever think about playing college basketball. I could not defend *anyone*, and that was the best part of my game! I could not dribble past *anyone*! Moreover, I could not get my shot off without getting blocked. I could not score, rebound, or even pass without turning the ball over the majority of the time. To make matters worse, there was one common denominator during scrimmages or cutthroat competitions: The team that had Pingel *always* lost. When Coach Wayne Rasmussen announced which color, or team, you were on for practice—everyone quickly looked to see what color shirt I received. If I were a blue, no one else wanted to be a blue. If your team lost a scrimmage or competition, you ran sprints. Let us just say that I helped some of the guys get in great physical condition that season. One lesson I learned that first fall of college life is that if you want to play college basketball, you probably need to play high school basketball first.

Did I mention that my teammates *hated* me?

I can joke about it today, but the icy glares, hollering, isolation, and loneliness I endured from my teammates that season hurt and cut deep. Even now, as I reflect as a middle-aged adult, I can still *feel* the loneliness, pain, and trauma of that season. Of course, I knew "that for those who love God all things work together for good" (Romans 8:28). God did indeed use that painful experience and laid it on my heart to make a promise to myself: If I ever got the opportunity to coach my own team someday, I would make sure that every player knew he or she was a child of God who could add value to the team experience. We would go out of our way to welcome and befriend *every* player on the team, no matter how talented.

Adding insult to injury that season, Coach Rasmussen—a great coach, pastor, and wonderful Christian man who would later officiate at my wedding—happened to confuse my name with another freshman (who would eventually be one of my roommates), Mark Poellot. Whenever Poellot made a mistake, Rasmussen would scream "Pingel! Pingel!!!! Come on, Pingel! Pingel, what are you doing?! Get your head in the game, Pingel!" Conversely, on the rare occasion when I actually executed something well in practice, Rasmussen would shout out, "Nice job, Poellot! That a way to stay after it, Poellot!" I made a mental note to myself: when you get your own team someday, spend a little extra cash and get the players' names printed on the back of their practice jerseys.

One day during a Christmas break practice, Coach Rasmussen brought the team together at midcourt. He asked every player to say something positive about another player. My heart rate suddenly increased and I wondered: Who is going to get stuck trying to say something nice about the walk-on who makes everyone else run? Dan Hueller, our gregarious, fun-loving, live-and-let-live senior center, was that man. The normally verbose Hueller struggled with silence for a moment, and then stated very earnestly, "Ping does a good job reversing the ball on the perimeter." Not exactly Hall of Fame induction speech material, but I'm convinced his words were the kindest and sweetest ever spoken on the Concordia Mequon campus. I actually had the nerve to thank him for his generous words after practice, and he could not have been more gracious: "You do a good job, Ping," he told me, "and you're actually getting better."

While I learned a ton about basketball and coaching that season, Dan Hueller's complimentary words are what I remember and cherish most. God certainly provided another leadership lesson for me: Never underestimate the power and long-term impact of kind words and specific compliments. Remember to raise the praise, encourage one another, and build one another up (1 Thessalonians 5:11).

Repeated shoulder dislocations, which forced corrective surgery, and new opportunities (I accepted the Sports Information Director position at CUW) led me to end my basketball playing days at the start of my sophomore year. Coach Rasmussen graciously allowed me to observe every practice and learn how to teach the game, motivate players, scout, and coach from the bench from an insider's perspective. His influence and impact on my life were significant. Later, when I became a basketball coach, I made my own adjustments and innovations to be sure, but most of what I did in practice and games in the early years of my coaching career originated from Coach Rasmussen.

I do not like to brag, but Rasmussen once told me that out of the five worst basketball players he ever coached, I was the best. His dry sense of humor was yet another endearing feature of his coaching repertoire.

Immediately after graduating from CUW, I entered graduate school at Marquette University to study early American history. During my graduate studies, I also had the opportunity to coach the boys JV basketball team at Martin Luther High School in Greendale, Wisconsin. Craig Mellendorf, who had been a former player and assistant coach under Wayne Rasmussen when I attended CUW, was the head coach at Martin Luther. He generously asked my roommate at the time, Jim Juergensen, and I to join his staff. We were thrilled for the opportunity. Craig was one of the most passionate and intense coaches you could ever know.

Under Craig's leadership and direction, I learned much about creating and developing a program blueprint, getting players to focus on nutrition, being relentless in the pursuit of goals and objectives, and perfecting the art of taping ankles! Craig gave me my first opportunity to coach my own team, and I am grateful for the trust he placed in me.

In the fall of 1994, having completed graduate school, I accepted a call to teach social studies at Mayer Lutheran High School and coach the freshman boys' basketball team. Due to limited gym space, the freshman team had to practice two blocks away from the high school in a run-down, rickety "community center" gym. Even though the floor was slippery and hard, the rims were tight and often had no nets, and the close walls had no padding behind the baskets, I absolutely *loved* coaching my team in the community center because the isolation inhibited distractions. This first real solo coaching experience became my basketball incubator. The challenge profoundly motivated me, and I gained invaluable experience organizing and running my own practices, dealing with parents, and coaching in a very competitive basketball environment all on my own.

Out of all the coaches I have ever observed, no one was a better motivator of his players than Jack Pallas at Mayer Lutheran. Jack truly loved "his kids," and they knew he did. Every Saturday morning during the season, Jack was interviewed on a local sports radio show (a big deal at the time in Minnesota). On his way to and from his interview, Jack would stop by and visit three or four of his players' homes and their families. His gregarious personality and enthusiasm, laugh, and sense of humor endeared him to these fine folks. He took time to be with them, and they appreciated it. Jack received more free breakfasts and lunches than any other person I know. Since his players liked, respected, *and* trusted him, he could challenge and push their competitive will. Watching Jack spend so much intentional time with these families impressed me and left an indelible mark on how I wanted to lead a program.

Another key leadership lesson I learned by observing Jack was the importance of confidence. Jack's players honestly *believed* they were better than they really were. There were many times I watched the opposing team warm up and anticipated a loss by twenty-five points only to see our team play way above our talent level and pull off the upset. Certainly, Jack knew the limitations each of his players possessed, but I never heard him say a negative word to a kid or tell them what they *could not* do. He made his players *feel* like excellent high school players, and then perform like it too. "I'm not going to tell them they really aren't this good," Jack told me once with a smile after an upset win. Right before the start of every varsity game, Jack would give the team the same pronouncement and instruction: "Okay, we're starting out in full-court man-to-man defense!" Most of the teams we competed against were quicker and faster than us, but our players did not know it. If Coach Pallas said we could play full-court pressure defense, our players believed they could do so too. Jack did not rely on scouting reports or informing his players of the caliber of the opponent. Whoever we played and no matter the talent gap, the *confident* Mayer Lutheran Crusaders were going to get after it and give them everything they had.

Head Coaching Faith Applications

In the fall of 2000, I became the head coach of the Mayer Lutheran Crusaders girls' varsity team. And while I did not know this at the time, I had begun a five-year tour of duty that would provide some of the most transformative faith and leadership experiences of my life. God truly had grand plans for me.

People frequently ask me, what are the differences in coaching girls and boys? For one, girls smell a whole lot nicer than guys, for sure. Second, they give you presents and baked goods for Christmas. Boys do not even think about giving their coach a Christmas gift. Third, while guys have a tendency to over-shoot, girls have a tendency to over-pass. Generally, you have to constantly exhort and discipline girls to take the open shot or shoot when they make an aggressive drive to the hoop. Finally, I learned to never cut kind and/or popular kids from the team since they always boosted student attendance at the games!

Over the next five years, the Mayer Lutheran Crusaders achieved a winning record and earned two conference championships. After having players in the system for four years, we went 22–3 and were ranked as high as number two in the state (division four). In my fifth and final season as a varsity head coach, we advanced to the Minnesota State Tournament—an appearance no Mayer Lutheran girls' team had achieved for more than three decades. To have been a part of those teams remains a cherished memory and honor. Hard as we worked for those accomplishments, however, they are not the experiences that mean the most to me today.

Time and space do not allow me to share every special memory, event, and relationship that remains embedded in my heart and mind from those five special years. Indeed, I replay and reflect on those special and specific moments almost daily. The best memories revolve around the relationships I had with the players and managers. Jill, Julie, Kelli, Sara, Christie, Erin, Liz, Jenny, Josi, Kristin, Karla, Amber, Rachel, Kristin, Jenny, Cally, Thea, Leah, Laurie, Melissa, Amie, Trish, Amanda, Amanda, Erica, Heidi (and so many more!) are just names to the reader, but to me they remain special young ladies who made a significant impact on my life. I loved those girls and their families. I stay in touch with many of them through social media, but certainly miss seeing or talking to them more often.

Profoundly grateful for the platform God gave me and wanting to be a successful and faithful *Christian* coach, I focused the Mayer Lutheran Crusaders on two scorecards. Yes, we were surely going to compete on the secular scoreboard for conference and sectional titles, but I also wanted the girls to see that our program would be invested in spiritual growth and relationships—with each other and, most important, with our Savior, Jesus Christ. Since Jesus had done all the salvation work on the cross and claimed victory over sin, death, and the power of the devil, we could not lose on this spiritual scorecard. He remained our captain, coach, and the Christ! Knowing Jesus meant we were winners *every day*, and being a redeemed sinner and winner changes everything.

Early on in my coaching journey, especially since I inherited a team that went 8-16 the season before, I learned that kids crave feedback, especially positive feedback. So, after each game, I typed a few paragraphs for each player on the team, and gave them feedback on how they had been practicing and competing in games, their progress on skill development, how they could improve, and their overall attitude and leadership in school. In addition to the basketball feedback, I included motivational quotes and Scripture passages—all personalized to the player's specific faith walk. I prayed that the Holy Spirit would fill their spiritual cups. The players had to store all these reports in a red binder so they could refer back to them frequently. These reports took an incredible amount of time to produce. I often stayed up till 1:00 a.m. after a game to get these done so I could hand them out to the girls the next day. Instant, caring, Christian feedback—on paper—was one of the things, I hoped, would set me apart as a coach. More important, I wanted the girls to know I cared about both their player development *and* faith development. After all, Jesus had already made them winners, and they would hear that every day in our program.

Over the next five years, we won often (87–38 overall). Our basketball program blossomed because the girls committed and dedicated themselves to skill improvement and team excellence. More important, we grew in our relationships with one another and, especially, with our Lord and Savior, Jesus Christ.

In addition to the championships and wins, God blessed me in more important ways. As the Holy Spirit continued to work on my heart, I began to see so many faith applications from my basketball coaching experiences. Many of these faith applications will appear in the devotions of this book, but a few coaching moments and experiences stand out as seminal moments in my own faith journey and indelible faith applications for me yet today.

The most difficult loss I ever experienced was in a sectional final game against Christ Household of Faith (CHOF). I believe my poor team preparation during the week prior to the game was the reason we lost. I did not properly prime my team for a physical, no-whistles-blown, playoff game of that magnitude. Today I still shudder at how easy and laid back I made our practices in the days leading up to that big game. Wanting my players to be fresh, healthy, and relaxed, I unintentionally sowed the seeds of passiveness and lethargy. Knocked in the teeth by the much more physical CHOF team from the opening tip, we never recovered. Even after a gallant comeback, we lost 45–40 (I still remember the score). Our record was 22–2 going into that game, and I truly believed God had blessed us with state-caliber talent and potential. Humbled, humiliated, and hurt, I felt responsible for the loss. *I would never have a team so underprepared and play so soft again.*

Of course, I did not know it at the time, but the following season would be my final as a varsity head coach and, as God would unpack it, the Mayer Lutheran Crusaders would get a rematch game in the playoffs against CHOF. During the year, I purchased and wore a CHOF T-shirt twice a week to practice. The girls hated it, which is why I modeled it. While I told them that I did not want them to forget the pain and devastation they felt after last year's playoff loss, the truth is I wore it so that I would not forget how inadequately I had prepared my team for the playoffs in the previous season. During the week before the sectional playoff game with CHOF, I swallowed my whistle and had the girls go to war in practice. To prepare for CHOF's stingy matchup zone, for example, I made the girls play five-against-seven. I ordered the two extra girls in the simulated matchup zone to incessantly and relentlessly foul the ball handler and cutters. My starters were almost hacked to death in practice leading up to the rematch game. I wanted them plenty toughened up. If they got stripped, turned the ball over, or complained about a foul, they did pushups or ran sprints by decree of a very Caesar-like and, at the moment, unpopular head coach.

Bloodied, beaten, but mentally and physical fortified and prepared, the girls were plenty tired of hearing about CHOF and seeing the CHOF T-shirt modeled by their coach. Displaying tenacity, toughness, and confidence, we defeated a talented and experienced CHOF team in the rematch playoff game. Without a doubt, it was one of the most satisfying moments for the girls and for me as a coach. The next day, the girls made me turn in my CHOF T-shirt. I'm told it wasn't pretty what they did with it in the locker room. We eventually won another playoff game and advanced to the state tournament, certainly a highlight for any coach or team. While we lost to a great opponent in a well-played game at state, we held our heads high and were honored to have represented our school at the state tournament for the first time in three decades.

The faith applications of that final season were many. To be candid, I thought my 22–3 team had more talent and played better defense. In my mind, they were the state-caliber team. Alas, life did not go according to my plan, but my 21–8 team *did* reach the promised land of hardwood. God had blessed them with great leadership skills, determination, and good timing. Today I reflect back on those last two seasons and realize that you never know when or where God is going to place you to do His bidding. His timing is always perfect. You might work hard and think you deserve rewards or the fruits of your labor (like I did for that 22–3 team), but God has other, better plans in mind for you. He certainly did for me.

One final Christian leadership lesson that God placed on my heart during my varsity coaching years is the realization that *every* kid you coach is an *intentional* gift God has placed in your life. I know this sounds Pollyannaish and warm and fuzzy, but I truly believed God put every student-athlete on my team and under my care for a reason.

This realization, among others, led me to make a decision, in only my second year of varsity coaching, to play at least ten girls in every game—two or three more players than most conventional coaches play. The reasons for making this a part of my coaching philosophy were many: (1) Because of my own experience, I had a heart for kids who did not receive much, or any, playing time. I wanted as many players as possible to get into the game and let them feel more direct ownership in the team; (2) If players knew they would play, I believed they would practice harder, and this reality would make our entire team better; (3) Let's be honest, playing more kids kept more parents happy; (4) We could wear teams down playing up-tempo pressure defense and keeping everyone fresh.

In all honesty, playing ten girls a game might have cost me a win or two during the regular season, but the sacrifice was worth it to me. As much as I wanted to win, I also wanted more student-athletes to have a life-changing experience playing and contributing on an elite, high school basketball team. For me, this was one of the best philosophical decisions I ever made, and I have no regrets whatsoever. The girls may or may not remember how many games we won or if we captured a conference title, but I *know* each of them cherished the short window of opportunity they had to contribute to something special.

Playing more players also fit my Christian worldview and long-term perspective on athletics. Since all of my players were a part of the Body of Christ, why not demonstrate this through playing time. Not everyone played equal time, of course, but I worked hard and diligently to make sure at least ten girls saw game action. Moreover, while we tried to win on the secular scorecard, executing well on the faith scorecard—through team prayers, devotions, Bible studies, reflections on God's Word, witnessing the faith, and so on—remained the other crucial objective. Our program pursued both championships and meaningful relationships—with one another and with Christ.

In the spring of 2000, the Minnesota State High School Association recognized me as the Section IV, Class A, Girls Coach of the Year, the last year I ever officially coached a high school basketball team. I share this fact not to brag, but to tell you the award means little to me today—the plaque is buried somewhere in my basement for my kids to throw out someday after I pass away. One thing I do cherish, however, is the memory of our JV boys' coach commending me for the award in front of the faculty and staff at Mayer Lutheran High School. A basketball junkie and excellent coach himself, his earnest words of praise remain a warm memory, even today. This was yet another reminder of how public praise and affirmation remain powerful forces for any leader or coach to embrace and employ.

New Players and Team Members to Coach

One of the most difficult moments in my young life was resigning as head basketball coach. At an early summer meeting, I sobbed in front of my players as I told them I had accepted the Call to serve as Executive Director of their school. Leaving the head coaching position, with a team loaded with state experience and so much talent returning, was truly a gut-wrenching decision. Nonetheless, God had asked me to coach a new team, and I felt duty-bound to lead the faculty and staff of Mayer Lutheran High School.

For the next fifteen years—five at Mayer Lutheran High School and ten at Sheboygan Lutheran High School in Wisconsin—I served as one of God's coaches, an Executive Director, at two outstanding schools alongside wonderful colleagues in Christ. Along the way, I also had the opportunity to coach my son, Joshua, and his grade school and youth basketball teams, and watch and work out with my daughter, who enjoyed playing the game of basketball too.

Coaching helped prepare me for administration and leadership. As a coach, you cast a vision, create a plan, work the plan, interact with and motivate people, resolve conflicts, prioritize, listen, pay attention to detail, follow through, keep your promises, prepare, work hard, show resilience after hardship, and realize that you cannot please everyone all of the time.

Most important, as a *Christian* administrator, you joyfully embrace the spiritual responsibilities and Christian leadership opportunities God provides. You keep the main thing the main thing, and encourage your faculty and staff to do the same. You constantly look for and make faith applications with almost all school experiences, and you encourage your team to do the same in their classroom and other co-curriculars. You pursue success not only on the secular, academic, and social scorecards, which exist in schools and communities to be sure, but also on mission fruition and the faith scorecard. Inspired by the Holy Spirit and as a disciple of Christ, you coach your entire school community—administrators, teachers, support staff, parents, students, donors, volunteers, and community members. It takes a Christian coach and Christian team to influence a village.

Competent Christian coaches in all sports, however, are difficult to find, especially for the smaller Christian schools and organizations that lack the personnel and resources. In my experience, I often found coaches who were either competent but not familiar or comfortable with the Christian faith or who were wonderful men or women of God but not skilled or capable of excellent coaching. Unfortunately, Christian school administrators are often forced to hire and choose between competency and mission fit. So, at long last, this is where this book comes into focus.

Why I Wrote This Book

The truth is that there are not a lot of deep, substantive Christian devotional books for youth coaches. I know this because I have looked for years, wanting to give a Christian devotional book to the coaches we hired at our Lutheran high schools. Moreover, I found most general sporting devotional books to be trite and shallow. Perhaps they had one Bible verse and two simple, short paragraphs of general exposition. I wanted to write a devotional that nurtured *and* stretched the reader on both the secular side of athletics and the faith side of life. This is why you will note several Bible passages listed for each devotion: in order to intentionally teach something both on the secular side of sports as well as biblical truths and faith applications. *One Team, One Spirit: Inspiration for the Christian Coach* is for the following:

- ◎ Seasoned and mature Christians who love coaching youth sports *and* want to grow in their faith.

- ◎ Christians who coach but are not always sure how to share their faith or who feel less confident in sharing or teaching the faith with their student-athletes.

- ◎ Coaches who may or may not have a strong Christian background or familiarity but who love sports and desire to grow in their own faith.

- ◎ Administrators and athletic directors who hire competent coaches but do not have resources to share to encourage these coaches in their spiritual development or faith walk.

- ◎ Parents, athletes, and fans who simply love sports *and* their Lord and Savior, Jesus Christ.

- ◎ Those who love youth sports and Christian life applications that can be made from athletics.

As many adults coach multiple sports, or even simply enjoy each sport season throughout a typical school year, this book is broken up into three seasons—fall, winter, and spring. Within each season, you will find fifteen devotions. Each devotion is made up of three sections: the main message for the sports enthusiast or coach, "A Devotion from the Coach to the Athletes," and "A Prayer for the Athletes." The first section speaks directly to the coach or reader, for his or her own personal and spiritual growth.

Included are several Bible verses to meditate upon, and each verse directly relates to the content of the devotion. Since faith comes by hearing the Word of God (Romans 10:17), plenty of Scripture is embedded throughout this book. The second section, "A Devotion from the Coach to the Athletes," provides a user-friendly devotion that a leader, coach, or parent could read to his or her athletes in a team devotional setting. Perhaps you feel confident enough in your faith to read this section ahead of time and then talk extemporaneously to your team with your own talking points. That's great! On the other hand, perhaps you would feel more comfortable reading the devotion out loud as written, adding anything you feel moved to add or that might be pertinent to the devotional material. Then this is the devotional book for you too! The third section, "A Prayer for the Players," offers a prayer you can use, if you are unsure or uncomfortable leading one on your own, as it relates to the topic or devotion. Thorough, substantive, and filled with delightful anecdotes and coaching scenarios to stir a sports junkie, this book was designed and written for coaches and fans, particularly of upper elementary, middle school, high school, and even the collegiate level.

Writing *One Team, One Spirit* was a labor of love. In fact, the production of much of this work took place during my son's senior year and my daughter's freshman year of athletics at Sheboygan Lutheran High School. Almost every night, after watching one of their games or competitions, I came home with a new idea and faith application. God is still using athletics to shape me as his instrument and disciple. How about you?

My prayer is that you may grow closer to Jesus, find inspiration in God's Word, and take the faith applications and Christian leadership challenges in these devotions to heart. Time is winding down, and your student-athletes are looking to you for leadership. They need a coach, a Christian coach, to lead the way, so take a time-out to be in God's Word, where He speaks truth and life to you. Draw up a plan. You can't lose because Jesus has already won. Well done, good and faithful coach.

FALL

Practice Gear, Shoes, and Uniforms— Oh My!

Finally, be strong in the Lord and in the strength of His might. Put on the whole armor of God, that you may be able to stand against the schemes of the devil. For we do not wrestle against flesh and blood, but against the rulers, against the authorities, against the cosmic powers over this present darkness, against the spiritual forces of evil in the heavenly places. Therefore take up the whole armor of God, that you may be able to withstand in the evil day, and having done all, to stand firm. Stand therefore, having fastened on the belt of truth, and having put on the breastplate of righteousness, and, as shoes for your feet, having put on the readiness given by the gospel of peace. In all circumstances take up the shield of faith, with which you can extinguish all the flaming darts of the evil one; and take the helmet of salvation, and the sword of the Spirit, which is the word of God, praying at all times in the Spirit, with all prayer and supplication. To that end, keep alert with all perseverance, making supplication for all the saints. (Ephesians 6:10–18)

FOR THE COACH

Many players love to be on a team because of the apparel, shoes, and uniforms. Cool-looking practice gear, finely designed warmups, specialty team T-shirts with catchy logos and inspirational quotes, new color-coordinated shoes, sporty backpacks and duffel bags, and trendy headbands and sweatpants are often part of the privilege and luxury bestowed to each player on a team. Certainly, team apparel and shoes often require a considerable financial outlay for parents—something coaches need to be cognizant of when determining needs versus wants. To be sure, players need shoes, practice jerseys, and uniforms to exist and function as a team. In addition, they provide a measure of status. Wearing a school's colors and uniform is a great honor and privilege.

Most important, practice gear, uniforms, warmups, and shoes help foster a team identity. This is why so many coaches want to see their athletes practicing in club team or school colors—unity and identity are almost always at the forefront of such thinking. Practice jerseys and uniforms make a statement. What you put on and wear says a lot about you as an individual, team, and program.

The Bible tells us that Christians are to put on "the whole armor of God" in their cosmic duel with sin and Satan. Disciples of Christ wear the "belt of truth" and "breastplate of righteousness." Their shoes make way to share the "gospel of peace." When Satan attacks and attempts to pull us away from our Lord, God calls His followers to "take up the shield of faith," put on the "helmet of salvation," and live by "the sword of the Spirit, which is the word of God" (Ephesians 6:10–18). Now that is a uniform!

Sadly, too many people today want to look good without actually putting in the work to be good. Even the best-looking uniforms do not help your team win one point, score one goal or touchdown, or take one second off your athletes' times. Looking good is fine, but being good is a whole different matter! Even more important, we know that as Christians we soil and stain our daily uniforms with hypocrisy, sin, and selfish behavior.

The good news is that God, through Jesus' death and resurrection, has given you and your players a new uniform and life-saving spiritual apparel. Your identity and theirs comes from Christ. Though our sins were like scarlet, they are now, because of Jesus, white as snow (Isaiah 1:18). (This does not mean your uniforms have to be white by the way.)

So dress up your athletes in the full armor of God. Make sure their shoes take them to church to receive God's grace. Give them devotions and warmups embroidered and pressed with God's Word. Encourage them to live a life that reveals their identity in Christ as well as a life that witnesses and shares the Good News with others. Help your players not only *look* good but, by God's grace, *be* good in Christ.

A DEVOTION FROM THE COACH TO THE ATHLETES

Come now, let us reason together, says the LORD: though your sins are like scarlet, they shall be as white as snow. (Isaiah 1:18)

One of the neat things about playing on an athletic team is all of the cool athletic gear you get to wear. Whether it is new shoes, wristbands or headbands, team T-shirts, backpacks, practice shorts, warmups, or whatever—it is fun to wear and bear our school colors and team name. I hope you know what an honor and privilege it is to wear our uniform and colors on game days. There are millions of boys and girls around the world who will never experience the thrill of wearing any kind of game-day attire. When you don our practice gear or put on our uniform, we show people that we are a team—that is our identity. We represent and stand for something special, so make sure you take care and keep that uniform pure and clean!

As Christians, we understand that our sins put us in a uniform of filthy rags (Isaiah 64:6 NIV). Jesus, however, purchased new spiritual uniforms for us with His own life. He cleaned our filthy life uniform and washed away our unrighteousness. He gave us a brand new righteous life, a clean heart—a spiritually bleached uniform. He made our sins, which were like scarlet, turn white as snow (Isaiah 1:18). And God gave us some really cool and crucial spiritual gear too—"the belt of truth . . . the breastplate of righteousness . . . shoes for your feet . . . the shield of faith . . . the helmet of salvation, and the sword of the Spirit, which is the word of God" (Ephesians 6:10–18). I hope those shoes get you to church every week so you can hear the Word of God and remember that your sins are forgiven. This full armor of God is an exceptional and miraculous spiritual uniform, and it will protect you from sin, death, and the power of the devil. You cannot find or purchase the full armor of God online or at some specialty store. You have done nothing to receive it and can do nothing on your own to get it. You and I have received this undeserved uniform of grace, this armor of God, because God loves you and wants you on His team both now and for all of eternity.

I pray that you wear this special uniform—the full armor of God—and wear it well not just this season, but every season for the rest of your life.

A PRAYER FOR THE ATHLETES

Dear heavenly Father,

Our identity comes from You. We are redeemed saints—Your sons and daughters—thanks be to Jesus. He washed away our filthy rags of sin on the cross of Calvary. We give thanks that our sins, which were like scarlet, are now white as snow. Empowered by Your grace and the Holy Spirit, inspire and strengthen us to wear the full armor of God as our daily uniform and give testimony of Your love.

In the name of the Father, the Son, and the Holy Spirit. Amen.

Parents'
Meeting

For there is no distinction: for all have sinned and fall short of the glory of God, and are justified by His grace as a gift, through the redemption that is in Christ Jesus. (Romans 3:22–24)

FOR THE COACH

You never get a second chance to make a first impression, so, at your early-season or preseason parent meeting, make sure you thoroughly prepare to win the hearts and minds of parents with caring, forthright, Christ-centered sincerity. Of course, you must talk about team expectations, goals, communication, practice schedule, transportation logistics, and all the other issues and details that allow your program or team to run smoothly and effectively. The always daunting issue of playing time for players must be directly addressed too. While coaches focus on the whole team, parents generally focus on the most important player on the team—their child. Therefore, coaches and parents often have conflicting interests when it comes to winning and playing time. Most parents simply want their child to be happy, and happiness usually correlates with playing time. Most coaches generally want to win and realize that they cannot play everyone equal minutes to do so.

Whatever the topic, spend the majority of your parent-meeting playing offense and reaching out to build relationships. Establish an open atmosphere of communication and dialogue. Put the parents in a semi-circle or circle and sit down and converse directly with them. Be forthright and tell them that you want their support. Remind them that you are an imperfect coach teaching imperfect student-athletes who were born from imperfect parents. In self-deprecating style, open up the floor to anyone who wants to argue with the fact that you are a sinful human being and a coach who makes mistakes. You might get a chuckle or smile out of them. Just as you do not expect their children to be perfect, they should not expect the coach to be perfect either. Ask that they practice and follow Matthew 18:15—"If your brother sins against you, go and tell him his fault, between you and him alone"—when conflicts arise. Coaching and teaching their children is made easier and more effective when both the parents and coach work together in Christian harmony.

Since the season is long, remind the parents that mountaintop and valley experiences are bound to come for the team and for their child, just like in real life. One thing you can promise the parents is "that for those who love God all things work together for good" (Romans 8:28). Their student-athlete will learn valuable life lessons throughout the season.

Finally, tell your parents that one of the joys of coaching is building relationships that last beyond the season. You want their child to have a great experience during the season, but you also want to build a wonderful, long-term relationship with their child, and with them too.

Of course, some parents will wear scowls, fold their arms, roll their eyes, and refuse to respond to your heartfelt outreach. If they sit back in their zone, go ahead and push the ball up the floor, spike it, hit the tight end, run through the chute, and knock down your putt. Show them you are confident, in command, and have a God-pleasing plan.

End your parent meeting with a heartfelt prayer—for the parents who are raising their children in the nurture and admonition of the Lord, for their children whom they are entrusting to you for Christian leadership and guidance, and for you the coach—that you may lead in a God-pleasing manner and truly focus on the life-lessons that will last beyond the season. If you are really feeling gutsy, ask a parent to pray for *you* in front of the group. Tell them you will need plenty more as the season goes on. A parent prayer before the season can be a powerful moment.

Successful and faithful Christian coaches have terrific relationships with their players *and* their players' parents. Be a leader and make yourself vulnerable first. Dialogue with them. Admit that you are not perfect. Ask for their prayers and support. Get them to laugh with you in the joy of the Lord. Show them your enthusiasm. Your confidence comes from Christ. A winning season is already underway.

A DEVOTION FROM THE COACH TO THE PARENTS

"This is the day that the LORD has made; let us rejoice and be glad in it." (Psalm 118:24)

I think the psalmist was referring to the beginning of our sport and season—how about you? Thank you all so much for coming to this parent meeting as we get set to kick off our season.

I want to start by thanking you for putting your trust in me and sharing your kids with me for the next few months. I hope they are looking forward to this adventure as much as I am.

Right now, I want to share with you some of the nuts and bolts of the team or program, talk about touchy issues like playing time and how to handle conflict, but also impart the vision of our team and what it means to be a Christian student-athlete, using the platform God has given us to be salt and light in this world.

No one involved with this team or program—not the coach, not the players, not the parents—is perfect. All of us are sinners, and we need to remember that, especially when things get tough or emotional.

The good news is that while all of us are sinners, we share a common faith in that we are redeemed sinners. Romans 8:28 says that "we know that for those who love God all things work together for good." No matter what happens this season to the team or to your child, God is in control. He is working out a plan for each of us, a plan that is for good. God tells us in 1 Thessalonians 5:11, "Therefore encourage one another and build one another up, just as you are doing." I can promise you there will be ups and downs, high points and low points this season. Through it all, let us remember as Christians that we need to build up and encourage one another. We are all important, special, and loved, and we all have an important role to play in the Body of Christ, so let us invite God to bless our season together.

A PRAYER FOR THE PARENTS

Dear heavenly Father,

We have so much to thank You for, but tonight I am especially grateful for these parents. Please continue to send Your Holy Spirit upon them, that they may continue to raise their children in the nurture and admonition of the Lord. Lord, we also pray that the student-athletes develop and grow as teammates and especially in their relationship with You. Finally, Lord, give me the wisdom, energy, and support to be the Christian coach and leader this team needs and deserves.

We ask this in the name of Jesus, our Rock and our Redeemer. Amen.

Stay in Your Stance

But in your hearts honor Christ the Lord as holy, always being prepared to make a defense to anyone who asks you for a reason for the hope that is in you; yet do it with gentleness and respect. (1 Peter 3:15)

FOR THE COACH

"Stay down!" "Get your butt down!" "Move your feet!" "Don't reach, just keep moving your feet!" "Get in an athletic position." "Stay in your stance!" Such are the common refrains and exhortations of coaches who demand excellence and proper athletic technique. Whether it be a basketball defender guarding a terrific offensive player, a back-row volleyball player preparing to receive a floater serve, a linebacker just before the snap of the football, a shortstop before the delivery of a pitch, or a sprinter right before the start of a short race on the track, exemplary athletes know the importance of getting in a good athletic stance. When players fail to get in a solid, leveraged athletic stance, bad things usually happen. They find themselves reacting too slowly to the play or out of position to make a play. They chase out of desperation instead of anticipating with confidence. They are unprepared and vulnerable to their opponent.

Just as disciplined players get in and stay in an athletic stance as they prepare for an opponent's offensive attack, Christians must stay in the Word of God if they are to be equipped for their "adversary the devil," who "prowls around like a roaring lion, seeking someone to devour" (1 Peter 5:8). Satan is looking to catch Christians unprepared and out of position.

In this postmodern age, numerous pagan philosophies, truth claims, and worldviews will vie not only for your student-athletes' allegiance, but also for yours. The purveyors of these philosophies will intimidate and coerce you and your student-athletes, who will be called and labeled intolerant bigots, flat-earthers, science-deniers, zealots, religious extremists, incompetent morons, and more. This persecution will hurt, cut deep, and lead to severe suffering for even the strongest of Christians. Satan will do anything to break apart the special relationship between a Christ-follower and Jesus. Therefore, we must prepare our young people for spiritual battle. They need to get in a solid spiritual stance to withstand Satan's offensive attack.

8

As a coach of young people—who often believe they are invincible or that Satan cannot touch them—remind your players to stay strong and in a solid spiritual position by receiving God's Word and grace anew each day. Model this with your players by reading from the Bible, or a devotion, before or after practice. If athletes do not train and practice their craft, their game becomes stale and atrophies. They do not grow in confidence or improve their skills.

Christians grow closer and strengthen their relationship with Jesus by talking to Him and listening to Him. Our relationship with Jesus never remains status quo. We are either moving toward Him or away from Him. When we pray to God, we are talking to Him. When we read God's Word, we are listening to Him. Not only does God's Word give us faith through the power of the Holy Spirit, but it also guides, directs, and protects us from the evil one, Satan, who is doing all he can to separate us from the love of God and His team of redeemed saints.

Coach and teach your players to get in a solid athletic stance so that they can be successful. More important, show and encourage your players to get in and stay in their spiritual stance by receiving God's Word daily and by being in church so that they can be faithful and obtain God's "crown of life" (Revelation 2:10).

All Scripture is breathed out by God and profitable for teaching, for reproof, for correction, and for training in righteousness, that the man of God may be complete, equipped for every good work. (2 Timothy 3:16–17)

Heaven and earth will pass away, but My words will not pass away. (Matthew 24:35)

The grass withers, the flower fades, but the word of our God will stand forever. (Isaiah 40:8)

A DEVOTION FROM THE COACH TO THE ATHLETES

When you get in and stay in a solid athletic stance, you are a more focused, athletic player—you anticipate better, you play with more confidence, and you are prepared and dialed in to the play and game action. When you get out of your stance, you are off-balance, out of position, reacting, and chasing—you are simply not ready to play and compete. The truth is that getting in and staying in your stance takes a great deal of discipline, commitment, and dedication on your part. If you do, however, the rewards as an individual, and as a team, are great.

As crucial as it is for you to stay in your stance so we can be successful on game day, you need to stay in a solid spiritual stance too. This is essential for your faith life. Satan loves it when we become lazy, sloppy, or careless with our spiritual lives. He loves it when we ignore the key fundamentals of our faith walk—things like daily devotions, Bible reading, and regular church attendance. If we do not take the time to listen to God's life-saving and life-changing Word, if we make other things more important than going to church regularly or praying to Him, then we will find ourselves unprepared, undisciplined, out of shape and position, and ultimately defeated in this tough and fallen world we live in. None of us could make the varsity spiritual team on our own. As children of God, we are able to withstand the devil's attacks because of the power of the Holy Spirit, who daily renews us and keeps us in our spiritual stance.

Stay in your stance when it comes to your faith. Listen to Jesus and His Word. Talk and pray to Him. By God's grace, keep the faith and win the crown of life.

A PRAYER FOR THE ATHLETES

Dear heavenly Father,

No matter how hard we try, we cannot overcome sin, death, and the power of the devil on our own. This is why we give thanks that You sent Your Son, Jesus, to die on the cross and forgive us of all our sins. May the Holy Spirit continue to strengthen us so that we might stay in a solid spiritual stance by praying daily, by reading Your Word daily, and by worshiping regularly.

In the name of the Father, the Son, and the Holy Spirit. Amen.

Home **Opener**

But our citizenship is in heaven, and from it we await a Savior, the Lord Jesus Christ, who will transform our lowly body to be like His glorious body, by the power that enables Him even to subject all things to Himself. (Philippians 3:20–21)

By wisdom a house is built, and by understanding it is established; by knowledge the rooms are filled with all precious and pleasant riches. (Proverbs 24:3–4)

FOR THE COACH

Tonight's competition has been a long time coming, and you are both excited and a little nervous. The home opener will be an eye opener for sure—hopefully in a good way. You and your team have been practicing for weeks, and now you finally get to play and compete in front of your home crowd. You know your athletes have been working hard, but nobody else really knows anything much about your team. This might be the first time the student-athletes' parents and countless other supporters of your school will see your team compete. And, well, you feel the pressure of that timeless coaching cliché: a team is a reflection of its coach.

Competing in your own gym, on your own field, is supposed to be an advantage for the home team, but the home opener brings a little added pressure. Your team should be more comfortable with the locker rooms, court or field dimensions, and the overall environment; your kids should play with more confidence and aggressiveness; there should be more supporters, parents, and fans in the bleachers ready to encourage and cheer for your student-athletes. The home team ought to perform better when they play or compete at home. And that is the point: No matter how well you have prepared your team, there are no guarantees. Even with all of these supposed home-court or home-field advantages, your team still has to execute.

One of the toughest lessons to impart to young people is that there are no guarantees in life either. Sometimes, despite our best efforts and perceived home-court or home-field advantages, our best effort simply is not good enough in this fallen world. As a coach, you know that you can scout, practice, and prepare in the most thorough manner possible for an upcoming opponent and still get beat. You can start all the right athletes and make all the proper coaching decisions during a contest and still get blown out.

We need to remind ourselves and the student-athletes we coach, however, that there is one constant and guarantee in life: Jesus. His death and resurrection for our salvation and the forgiveness of our sins already made history. The final score is impressive. Jesus won the battle over Satan and our sinful flesh, and it was not even close. On the cross of Calvary, when Jesus said, "It is finished" (John 19:30), Satan lost, and we by God's grace and mercy were declared the victors and were redeemed.

Athletes and coaches often say, when referring to their home field or home court, that they must defend their "house." Thanks to Jesus, your "citizenship is in heaven" (Philippians 3:20). In other words, heaven is your God-given house, your home. And it's packed with all the saints.

Until you are called home, you will be on the road—a stranger in this land. Nevertheless, the Bible encourages you to "press on toward the goal for the prize of the upward call of God in Christ Jesus" (Philippians 3:14). By God's grace, you can do this knowing that a glorious home-court and home-field advantage—heaven— awaits you, thanks be to Jesus. What a home opener and homecoming that will be!

A DEVOTION FROM THE COACH TO THE ATHLETES

But as for me and my house, we will serve the LORD. (Joshua 24:15)

In My Father's house are many rooms. If it were not so, would I have told you that I go to prepare a place for you? And if I go and prepare a place for you, I will come again and will take you to Myself, that where I am you may be also. (John 14:2–3)

Our home opener is here. It's always nice to compete at home. We are in our familiar surroundings and do not have to travel. Plus, I think it's really fun to compete in front of our fans and supporters—don't you? I would rather be encouraged and cheered for than booed.

There is this belief, too, that teams generally play or compete better at home for some of the reasons I already mentioned. At home, you get to defend your own "house" or home turf. Many of your classmates, friends, and fans have come out to encourage and support you. They really want to see you do well and be successful, so let's take advantage of competing at home, not just today or tonight for the home opener, but for every home contest on our schedule.

But as much as we might have an advantage at home, playing or competing on our home court, course, or field does not guarantee success or wins. There are no guarantees in life. I know this to be true. And you know this to be true. You can diligently study for a test for hours and still fail it. You can give a terrific interview and still not get the job. You can try to impress that certain guy or girl, and he or she still might say "no thank you" to a date or dance request. You can try to get along with your classmates or make new friends, but they still might not invite you to their parties. You can write an exemplary and professional essay and still not receive the scholarship. You can even pay your dues in practice and still not get the playing time you desire. I wish a win was guaranteed in our home opener, but it is not.

The only guarantee in life is that God loves you so much that He sent His one and only Son to suffer, die, and rise for you. Your sins are forgiven, and heaven—God's house—is your home.

Until God calls you home to check into His heavenly mansion someday, recognize that you have been given an incredible home-field or home-court advantage while living here on earth. You already know the victory you have in Christ, and no team, no opponent, no one can take that away from you. You cannot and do not have to do anything to earn or merit this victory—it's yours because of Jesus. That's why you can compete in a home opener with no fear and live your life with no fear. God has already opened up His home to you through the Door, His Son, Jesus Christ. That's the home opener, or the heaven opener, that really counts.

A PRAYER FOR THE ATHLETES

Dear heavenly Father,

We are so excited and thrilled for the opportunity to compete for the very first time this season in front of our home crowd. Thank you for this special day.

Of course we want to win, but more than that, Lord, we want to give glory and honor to You with how we play and conduct ourselves. Help us to use the gifts and talents You have given us to the fullest and to give a good testimony of Your love for us.

In the name of the Father, the Son, and the Holy Spirit. Amen.

Finishing Strong

Better is the end of a thing than its beginning, and the patient in spirit is better than the proud in spirit. (Ecclesiastes 7:8)

I have fought the good fight, I have finished the race, I have kept the faith. Henceforth there is laid up for me the crown of righteousness, which the Lord, the righteous judge, will award to me on that day, and not only to me but also to all who have loved His appearing. (2 Timothy 4:7–8)

FOR THE COACH

No matter the sport, all coaches want their teams to execute and play well all the way through to the end of the game or competition. When players sink birdie putts on their last three holes, pass several runners during the last eight hundred yards of a race, execute the two-minute offense and score a touchdown late in the fourth quarter, or win the shoot-out at the end of a double-overtime soccer match, coaches get excited and experience a deep sense of satisfaction. Their players executed during crunch time and, generally, when it mattered most.

One of the unique aspects of volleyball is that no matter how poorly a team plays up to a certain point in the match, they can still win the match if they outplay their opponent from that point forward. Your team could, for example, be down two games to none and behind 24–0 in game three of a five-set match but still win if your club outplays and out-executes the opponent for the remainder of the match.

Every sport is unique in its own way, but the game of volleyball provides a terrific opportunity and analogy to teach your student-athletes about the love of Jesus Christ and what He did for them on the cross over two thousand years ago. You see, spiritually, you and your players, because you are sinners, are down two games to none and 24–0 in game three of a five-set match with little hope of a heavenly comeback. In our fallen world, sin has crushed each of us. On our own, we are dominated by our sinful nature and sins in thought, word, and deed. We are demoralized. The deficit is too large to overcome, the score or record of sin too great for any possible or legitimate hope of a comeback. You and your players, all of us, need divine intervention and a Savior to change the logical outcome.

Substitution, please. Enter Jesus. He came down from heaven and took our place on the court of life and on the cross of Calvary. By His death and resurrection, He gave each of us victory over sin, death, and the power of the devil.

Great volleyball teams pass, set, and hit with discipline, consistency, and precision. Your Savior, Jesus Christ, did all of these things to perfection for your spiritual and eternal well-being. On the cross, He took on and took away all of your sins. When God looks down upon you, He does not see your sins but His Son, Jesus, interceding for you. You have been given a perfect *pass*, a get-out-of-hell pass, for all of your sins. Because of Jesus, you are perfectly *set* for eternity. God has many rooms and a place waiting for you in heaven (John 14:2–3). He also has grand plans for you here on earth before you are called to heaven. When Jesus shed His innocent blood for you, He *hit* and killed Satan's plan to separate us from God. He overcame and defeated our sinful nature, death, and the power of the devil. Pass, set, hit—Jesus turned your dire, sinful, dead life into a redeemed and righteous one. From the cross to the empty tomb, Jesus finished strong for you, your players, and all who call and know Him by name. You and Jesus are a great match, a match made complete in heaven.

A DEVOTION FROM THE COACH TO THE ATHLETES

When Jesus had received the sour wine, He said, "It is finished," and He bowed His head and gave up His spirit. (John 19:30)

One of the characteristics of a magnificent team is one that finishes strong. No matter what the circumstances, no matter what the score, no matter how we or you have played to a certain point, we finish strong. If we were playing volleyball and found ourselves in a three-game match having already lost game one and on the brink of defeat down 24–0 in the second game of a three-set match, we'd know we could still win by outplaying our opponent from that moment forward. In volleyball, it is all about how you finish a match that really counts.

In our spiritual lives and faith walk here on earth, it's all about how we finish too. Whenever your earthly life might end, what is really going to matter on your last day is whether you know Jesus Christ as Lord and Savior. Heaven is our home. Only Jesus can get you to heaven where there will be no more tears, no death, no pain, no mourning, no crying, and no sin. Heaven is perfect, paradise, and most important, heaven is the place where we will live with Jesus for all of eternity. That's finishing strong.

Whether we start out playing well or playing poorly, let's remember that how we finish the match is what really matters. We will never be perfect in our passing. We will never set every ball properly. We will hit some balls out of bounds and have others blocked or go into the net. No matter how hard we try, we will never play a perfect match. Life is the same way. No matter how hard we try, we will never live a flawless life and get to heaven on our own works and efforts. Only Jesus lived the perfect life on earth, and only Jesus can save you and me from our sins. The good news is that He loves you each just that much. He shed His innocent blood for you. You and I have been given a pass. Our salvation is set and assured. Jesus hit and crushed Satan, killed our sins, and scored a victory over death. "It is finished," Jesus declared on the cross (John 19:30). Inspired by Jesus' love and redemption, may we always finish strong in competition but, most important, in life.

A PRAYER FOR THE ATHLETES

Dear heavenly Father,

Teams and players who finish strong improve their chances of performing well or winning. In life, however, we could never overcome our sins without the grace and mercy You showed us through Your Son, Jesus Christ. Thank You for the cross and empty tomb. Thank You for sending Your Son to die for our sins and rise from the dead. Jesus finished strong. By God's grace and the power of the Holy Spirit, help us remain steadfast and strong in You, both now and forever.

In the name of the Father, the Son, and the Holy Spirit. Amen.

The Two Scorecards

But thanks be to God, who in Christ always leads us in triumphal procession, and through us spreads the fragrance of the knowledge of Him everywhere.
(2 Corinthians 2:14)

Have nothing to do with irreverent, silly myths. Rather train yourself for godliness; for while bodily training is of some value, godliness is of value in every way, as it holds promise for the present life and also for the life to come.
(1 Timothy 4:7–8)

FOR THE COACH

Most Valuable Player. Most-Improved Player. All-Conference. All-Area Team. Player of the Year. All-Tournament Team. All-State. Tournament Champ. Coach of the Year. Prep Athlete of the Week. Conference Title. Sectional and Regional Championship. State Championship.

Anyone who has ever played or coached would be thrilled to find success in one or more of these marks of distinction. Pursuing wins and championships are worthy goals. Moreover, there is nothing wrong with striving for individual success and peer recognition. Competition, with the proper perspective, is a healthy endeavor and encourages good stewardship of the various gifts, talents, and treasures God so graciously and generously bestowed on each one of us. Furthermore, people notice and pay attention to success and winners. An excellent team or an outstanding athlete gains access, status, and the opportunity to witness and share the Christian faith all the more. For all of these reasons and more, you should push your team to achieve on the secular scorecard. Go for it!

Since the pressure and status of winning and achieving individual accomplishments are so pervasive and lauded in our culture today, losing can become an anathema and miserable mark on one's identity. When you lose, parents question and openly criticize your competency and coaching techniques. Your perceived shortcomings as a coach might be discussed publicly and even become a trend on social media, depending on how high-profile you or your team is. You might even lose your job if things do not improve.

In addition, your players feel the pressure to achieve and succeed on the secular scorecard too. Losing teams often experience disdain or, even worse, ambivalence from the school community or greater public. Classmates and peers openly mock and ridicule their "friends" for their apparent lack of skill and dismal performances. People outside your team or program do not give credit or praise for how hard your players work or how much they improve, because losing teams are simply not that compelling. Losing means you are a loser.

As a Christian coach, you must teach your student-athletes the two scorecards—the secular scorecard and God's scorecard. And here is the good news: Your team can win at both! In fact, because of Jesus, your team has already won on the most important one.

God's scorecard is not about earthly success, the wins and losses and individual accolades, but about God's faithfulness, grace, and mercy toward us. On His scorecard, you and your players are already eternal winners—redeemed sinners—cleansed by the blood of Christ. In Christ is the victory!

When you lead your team in Bible study or devotions, when you pray with them every day in practice, when you encourage them to be faithful in their church attendance and study of Scripture, when you remind them of Jesus' love for each and every one of them, you are reinforcing the truth that your players are special children of God and have already received the ultimate prize—the forgiveness of sins and a place in heaven. That's how winning looks on God's scorecard!

Christian coaches and players, like anyone, can lose track of what's important, the ultimate goal. Therefore, go ahead and strive for success on the secular scorecard, but ask God to guide and remind you to stay focused on His scorecard each and every day too. Coach, play, practice, and live like a winner and redeemed sinner—because that is who you are. Thanks be to Jesus!

A DEVOTION FROM THE COACH TO THE ATHLETES

Whatever you do, work heartily, as for the Lord and not for men, knowing that from the Lord you will receive the inheritance as your reward. You are serving the Lord Christ. (Colossians 3:23–24)

But thanks be to God, who gives us the victory through our Lord Jesus Christ. (1 Corinthians 15:57)

Vince Lombardi, the legendary Packer coach and the one after whom the Super Bowl trophy is named, is often quoted as saying, "Winning isn't everything; it's the only thing." What biographers actually think he said, however, is that "the will to win is the only thing."

Either way, Lombardi made a great point. We want to win and work hard to win. As long as people keep score or keep time, we want to win and achieve at a high level. The more we win or excel, the more people will pay attention to our team and wonder what makes us special. How fun is that!

More important than actually winning, striving to win can bring out the best in us. As Christians, God calls on each of us to be good stewards, to focus on using all of our God-given gifts to the fullest. If you truly work hard to improve, be a good teammate, and do the best you can with what God has given you—that is winning. Beyond our team goals, many of you have set individual goals too, so be a leader and strive to improve your skills and performance each and every day. You can do it, and I hope you do!

On our team and in our program, however, there is more than one way to win. We have two scorecards that matter to us. The secular scorecard is what we just talked about, winning in competitions and achieving team and individual goals. The other scorecard is God's scorecard. God's scorecard is not about earthly or secular success, the wins and losses and individual accolades, but about God's faithfulness, grace, and mercy toward us. God's scorecard is about Jesus' win—His victory—over sin, death, and the power of the devil. On God's scorecard we are already winners because Jesus paid the price for our sins on the cross. Our sins are forgiven, and we did nothing collectively or individually to earn this victory. Our victory comes only from Christ.

So, every day in practice, let us work hard and strive to win and succeed on that secular scorecard. But let us also spend time focusing on God's scorecard by reading Scripture and devotions, encouraging each other to receive God's grace and Word in church, and lifting up our prayers to God daily. All of you should live like a redeemed champion today, a most valuable person and player, because that is who you are because of Jesus. By God's grace may you remember both scorecards and what Jesus did for you and how much He loves you each and every day this season and for the rest of your lives.

A PRAYER FOR THE ATHLETES

Dear heavenly Father,

Your Son was humbled and brutally hung on a cross on that first Good Friday. To the world He looked like a loser. But three days later, Jesus triumphantly rose from the dead. We give thanks that You sent Your Son to die on the cross and take away our sins. Jesus defeated sin, death, and the power of the devil once and for all. Thank You for taking us sinners and making us winners, redeemed for eternity.

In the name of the Father, the Son, and the Holy Spirit. Amen.

The Hammer and the Nails

Is not My word like fire, declares the Lord, and like a hammer that breaks the rock in pieces? (Jeremiah 23:29)

He Himself bore our sins in His body on the tree, that we might die to sin and live to righteousness. By His wounds you have been healed. (1 Peter 2:24)

FOR THE COACH

"Someone is gonna be the hammer, and someone is gonna be the nail. Be the hammer!" The hammer and the nail—these are words used by many football coaches across the country to instill an attitude of aggressiveness and physicality required in the sport. The hammer dictates and dominates the action and play. The nail absorbs and takes the punishment. One is aggressive, the other is passive.

Coaches in other fall sports use hammer and nail analogies too. In volleyball, players must stay on the "attack" and "hit" or "hammer" the ball home instead of gingerly tipping and dinking the ball over the net. In cross country, runners might hear their coach exhorting them to "drop the hammer" for the stretch run. Soccer players must play "tough as nails" in a very physical game without pads and hammer their penalty or shoot-out kicks home. In all of these sports, being aggressive, confident, and assertive remain key ingredients for athletic success.

One reason the hammer-and-nail analogy is so compelling and powerful to student-athletes is that everyone can relate to it. Almost everyone sees and experiences the power and force of a hammer. Many have even used a real hammer and accidentally hit their own finger or pounded too hard and damaged something they were hoping to create or fix. They also know that nails receive and absorb a tremendous impact. No one wants to be a nail. And here is another reality: If you decide not to be the hammer, then you will become the nail. You are either one or the other. Thus, in your sport, you are right and sound to teach your student-athletes to be the hammer!

In regard to our spiritual lives, however, the hammer and the nails take on quite a different meaning and provide wonderful analogies of faith for us to reflect upon. The truth is that more than two thousand years ago, our sins hammered *and* nailed Jesus Christ to the cross of Calvary. Jesus loved us so much that He went willingly to the cross to die for our sins, and hammers literally punched nails through His skin and bones and bound Him to a wooden cross.

Another way of looking at God's plan of salvation, however, is that Jesus became *both* the hammer and the nail. As a hammer, Jesus pounded and crushed sin, death, and the power of the devil one time for all time. As a nail, He absorbed and took on all of our sins and the sins of the world even though He was almighty, all-powerful, innocent, and perfect in every way. Both a hammer and nail are needed to stick or hold something in place. Jesus' death and resurrection will stick us, or place us, in heaven someday. Our sins have been nailed to the cross. We are forever bound and fastened to the blood of Jesus.

In most sports, you would rather be the hammer than the nail, so pound on your student-athletes to achieve and nail peak performance. More important, remind your players that Jesus was true man, true God, and a carpenter. He knew about hammers and nails. In God's plan of salvation, only Jesus could be the hammer and the nail. Only He could die and rise again, so that you might live forever, someday, in a heavenly mansion built for you.

A DEVOTION FROM THE COACH TO THE ATHLETES

By canceling the record of debt that stood against us with its legal demands. This He set aside, nailing it to the cross. (Colossians 2:14)

I have been crucified with Christ. It is no longer I who live, but Christ who lives in me. And the life I now live in the flesh I live by faith in the Son of God, who loved me and gave Himself for me. (Galatians 2:20)

Someone has to be the hammer, and someone has to be the nail! You know that is true in our sport. As the hammer, you are confident, physical, in position, strong, tough, aggressive, and ready to dictate to your opponent or set your own pace. As the nail, you are soft, passive, indecisive, and often reacting or waiting for your opponent to make the first move. Be the hammer and not the nail! I want a team full of student-athletes who are ready to hammer it home, to pound for great performance, and to nail their personal and team goals. If you act and perform in a passive or soft manner, then your opponent will sense that and become the aggressor in the competition. Of course, we want to play by the rules and always demonstrate good sportsmanship. You can do that and still be the hammer, not the nail.

Speaking of hammers and nails, do you remember that Jesus was a carpenter? Jesus knew all about hammers and nails throughout His earthly life, even right up to His last moments on the cross. In fact, hammers and nails were used for His crucifixion. We do not even want to imagine the physical pain and suffering He endured when those hammers and nails pierced his hands and feet and pinned Him on a cross.

While hammers and nails were used to crucify Him, the truth is our sins and the sins of the world nailed Jesus to the cross. He took on the hammers, nails, and all the sins of the world and yours, too, because He loved you that much.

The good news is that Jesus became both a hammer and the nail for you and me. Only Jesus could be both the hammer and the nail when it comes to our salvation. He pounded and hammered sin, death, and the power of the devil forever when He shed his blood for you. Instead of dying in your sins, Jesus absorbed your sins and nailed them to the cross. Our sins have been crucified in Christ, and Jesus now lives in each of us (Galatians 2:20). You are redeemed. Just as an effective carpenter might use a hammer and nails to fasten and bind something together, Jesus wants you, by the power of the Holy Spirit, to stick with Him.

On this team, I want you to be a hammer and not a nail. In your personal lives, though, remember that hammers and nails, by the blood of Christ, made your salvation possible. Jesus was more than a carpenter and nice teacher. He is your Savior.

A PRAYER FOR THE ATHLETES

Dear heavenly Father,

Thank You for taking the hammer and the nails on the cross of Calvary so that our sins would be forgiven. Only You could smash sin, death, and the power of the devil forever. Only You could nail our sins to the cross. Forgiven and redeemed, may we witness Your grace and love to others wherever we go and whatever we do.

In the name of the Father, the Son, and the Holy Spirit. Amen.

Breakaway

I appeal to you therefore, brothers, by the mercies of God, to present your bodies as a living sacrifice, holy and acceptable to God, which is your spiritual worship. Do not be conformed to this world, but be transformed by the renewal of your mind, that by testing you may discern what is the will of God, what is good and acceptable and perfect. (Romans 12:1–2)

Out of my distress I called on the LORD; the LORD answered me and set me free. (Psalm 118:5)

FOR THE COACH

There is no more exhilarating instant in a soccer match than a breakaway. Seeing a player separate herself from a pack of players and bear down on the goal is truly a thrilling and critical moment. The play develops quickly, sometimes seemingly out of nowhere, and ends in a blink of an eye. The action is scintillating and keeps you on the edge of your seat (or jumping up and down). Will she score, or will the goalie make an incredible save?

Beyond an exciting and thrilling moment, breakaways are often game-changers. One team can control the ball and dominate an entire contest, only to see the opposing team get one breakaway, score the goal, and win the match. You always seem to have a chance to win if you have a player who is capable of making a big play on a breakaway.

Others sports display their own breakaway moments. The cross-country runner who intentionally takes an early lead with a brisk pace sets the tone or sends a message that he is determined to win the race. Or maybe the runner conserves his energy until the last mile of a hilly course where he kicks into another gear and passes multiple runners on the way to a top-five finish. Volleyball teams that can turn a 7–7 game into a 20–7 breakaway deliver a demoralizing blow to the opponent. The receiver who can execute a double move on the outside and leave the defensive back in his wake receives the deep ball in stride. The basketball player who intercepts a lazy wing pass and sprints to the other basket makes an easy lay-up, his opponents too far behind to even get close for a block or defensive play. The golfer who birdies her last three holes defeats her opponent. In every sport, breakaways stand out and change the complexion of the athletic contest and bring beautiful bounty to a sports coach!

More important, there is another kind of breakaway that sets you apart. Born with a sinful nature and selfish desire, you were destined for hell and eternal damnation, "for the wages of sin is death" (Romans 6:23). In His infinite grace and mercy, however, God had a plan to redeem you, to free you from your own sinful thoughts, words, and deeds. He gave you a breakaway from your own sinful self. He sent His Son, Jesus, who died on the cross as a payment for your sins. Thanks to Jesus, you have been set free from your sins. Christ broke the chains that bound you to sin, death, and the power of the devil. By God's grace, you are way out in the clear with the ball and no defense or goalie to stop you from receiving the prize (1 Corinthians 9:24) of eternal life. What a score!

No matter how busy or demanding life gets, remember to break away from the world and receive God's Word and Sacraments in the worship service each and every week. Take the time for your own personal devotions, Bible study, and prayer. Your soul needs to be set free—to break away from the pack and daily grind—and find rest and peace in Christ. Remind your players to do the same. Better yet, show them how you make Jesus and God's Word a priority in your life. Good and God-pleasing things happen on breakaways.

A DEVOTION FROM THE COACH TO THE ATHLETES

So if the Son sets you free, you will be free indeed. (John 8:36)

But now that you have been set free from sin and have become slaves of God, the fruit you get leads to sanctification and its end, eternal life. (Romans 6:22)

I love it when I see one of you get a breakaway and bear down on the opponent's goal. Those moments do not happen all that often, so when they do I know we have a high-percentage opportunity to score and make a big play.

I do not know if you have thought about it, but good things usually come for teams in other sports, too, when they get a breakaway. Think about a basketball player who gets the steal at half court, which usually leads to an easy bucket on the other end. Or the cross-country runner who breaks away from the pack of runners during the last mile of a race. Or how about a wide receiver who gets behind the secondary and receives a beautiful pass, or a running back who breaks through the secondary on the way to a long touchdown run. Then, there is the volleyball team that runs off ten straight points to break the spirit or demoralize the other team. Or how about the golfer who sinks three straight one-putt birdies in competition to put the match out of reach. Good things usually happen in sports if you or our team manages to get a breakaway.

There is an even more important breakaway that I want you to remember and reflect upon today, and that is how Jesus made it possible for you to break away from sin, death, and the power of the devil when He shed His blood for you on the cross. On our own, we cannot shake our sinful nature or our sinful thoughts, words, and deeds. We are stuck in the middle of the pack, clumped together with all sinners. We are dead to sin or, as the Bible notes, "the wages of sin is death" (Romans 6:23). The only way we can escape the bondage of sin, the only way we can break free or break away from our own sinful flesh and the grip of sin is through our Savior, Jesus Christ. When He died on the cross, He paid the price for our sins—washed them away—so that we might have eternal life with Him in heaven. Thanks to Jesus, we have been given a breakaway from eternal damnation. We have been set apart; we are out in the clear with no defense or goalie to overcome and no kick necessary to make. Jesus already scored and won the victory for us. More than any playmaker, Jesus is our Savior.

A PRAYER FOR THE ATHLETES

Dear heavenly Father,

Thank You for sending Your Son, Jesus, to redeem and cleanse us from all of our sins. Only through His sacrifice have we made a breakaway and been set free from sin, death, and the power of the devil. By the power of the Holy Spirit, help us to remain steadfast in Your grace and mercy and continue to receive God's Word and Sacraments faithfully.

In the name of the Father, the Son, and the Holy Spirit. Amen.

Digs and Kills

A soft answer turns away wrath, but a harsh word stirs up anger. (Proverbs 15:1)

Gracious words are like a honeycomb, sweetness to the soul and health to the body. (Proverbs 16:24)

Let the words of my mouth and the meditation of my heart be acceptable in your sight, O LORD, my rock and my redeemer. (Psalm 19:14)

FOR THE COACH

Digs and kills remain two essential habits and skills of any successful volleyball team. You cannot play good defense and convert to offense without players who scrap and hustle to "dig out" the ball before it hits the ground. In the same manner, exemplary volleyball teams possess players who attack an opposing team with a ferocious spike or a strategically well-placed tip that cannot be returned. The importance of executing digs and kills is evident by the amount of time coaches spend on passing and hitting drills. Fans, too, recognize the significance of a terrific dig or momentous kill and applaud and cheer on players who execute these skills.

Unfortunately, there are different digs and kills that are not desirable nor inspirational in our daily walk here on earth. Verbal slights, harmful words, or digs—intentional or unintentional—often hurt the soul.

Our world can be a cruel, vindictive place to live. Perhaps you have endured verbal abuse or bullying, condescension, passive aggressive slights and emails, mockery, overbearing sarcasm, or outright hateful language. More than likely, especially in the Internet and social media age, your players have experienced the same.

This is one reason why your team needs to be a place where each one of your players is respected and valued as a special child of God.

How are you doing at monitoring the language and words players speak to each other on your team? Often times the digs and kills that hurt the most over the long haul are the ones that seem innocent or permissible at the time. A player may appear to be laughing along with the rest of the team at her assigned nickname, for instance, but is she masking or hiding her embarrassment, anger, or hurt? Be observant, too, of the star or more talented player who condescends or cuts down his teammates because they cannot compete as well as he can. As the Bible indicates, harsh or rash words cut like swords (Proverbs 12:18), and swords can maim someone, or worse, take their life.

We often think of the physical abuse Jesus endured on the way to the cross—the scourging, the crown of thorns, the actual crucifixion—but don't forget the verbal taunting, ridicule, sneering, mockery, and many words of derision He endured. Though He was true God and true man, perfect and innocent in every way, kind and merciful, Jesus was accused of being a blasphemer, lawbreaker, rebel, heretic, and false prophet. Mocked and scorned for being labeled the "King of the Jews," taunted and ridiculed for not freeing and saving Himself from the cross, Jesus heard and endured the worst of human nature through the deep scars of cutting words, lies, and disparagement. Even in His last moments, He could not escape the belittling words of a criminal on a cross who questioned His divinity.

As a Christian leader, you can set a different tone and climate for your team through your actions *and* words. More important, you know that it is the Word of God, by the power of the Holy Spirit, that gives us our faith. Words matter, especially God's words in Scripture, so discuss with your team how they should talk to one another. Share God's Word daily. Reflect on Scripture and devotional thoughts throughout your season. Pick a team Bible verse or theme and meditate on it each day. Lift up one another in prayer. Eliminate and do not tolerate any talk that hurts and does not inspire, encourage, or build up one another in the faith. Keep digging into God's Word and kill 'em with Christian kindness.

A DEVOTION FROM THE COACH TO THE ATHLETES

Jesus said . . . , "If you abide in My Word, you are truly My disciples, and you will know the truth, and the truth will set you free." (John 8:31–32)

Your word is a lamp to my feet and a light to my path. (Psalm 119:105)

Digs and kills—as far as volleyball play goes, we like these a lot! Seriously, volleyball coaches love it when they see their players diving on the ground and digging out a serve or a free ball.

Seeing that hustle and tenacity on display inspires the fans, your teammates, and your coach. In the same way, when someone hammers and puts down a rocket ball on the opposing team's side of the net, we like that! That gets us excited for sure! Every kill is a score for us. If we get lots of digs and kills, we have a wonderful opportunity to be successful on the court. That is why we will keep practicing both skills.

There is another set of digs and kills, however, that are not desirable or good. Every single one of us has been hurt by a cutting comment, a dig, whether it was intentional or unintentional. That old saying, "sticks and stones may break my bones, but words will never hurt me"—we know this statement is a lie. Perhaps you have said, written, or posted a dig at someone else and later regretted it.

The Bible tells us that harsh words "are like sword thrusts" (Proverbs 12:18) that seriously injure and can even lead to death. The human tongue is "unrighteous," capable of "staining the whole body," because it is "full of deadly poison" (James 3:5–8). Mean, harmful, passive-aggressive words, digs, can kill and crush the soul.

The Bible has a lot to say about verbal digs and kills and how we are to speak and treat one another:

◎ "If anyone thinks he is religious and does not bridle his tongue but deceives his heart, this person's religion is worthless" (James 1:26).

◎ "Let no corrupting talk come out of your mouths, but only such as is good for building up, as fits the occasion, that it may give grace to those who hear" (Ephesians 4:29).

◎ "Let your speech always be gracious, seasoned with salt, so that you may know how you ought to answer each person" (Colossians 4:6).

◎ "Be kind to one another, tenderhearted, forgiving one another, as God in Christ forgave you" (Ephesians 4:32).

Words make a deep impact. Think about it, Jesus was the *Word* that became flesh (John 1:14). We come to faith through hearing and receiving the Word of God. Words matter!

So let us be a team that encourages others through kind, loving words. Let's share God's Word so others may not feel the sting of verbal digs and soul kills, but inspiration, joy, forgiveness, peace, hope, and love. On the court, we work hard for digs and kills. Off the court, however, let's dig into God's Word and stop saying things that discourage, cut, or denigrate others. Let's kill 'em with Christian kindness instead.

A PRAYER FOR THE ATHLETES

Dear heavenly Father,

Forgive us when we say or do things that hurt or harm others. Instead of verbal digs that denigrate others, encourage and inspire us to hear, receive, and dig into Your life-changing and life-saving Word.

In the name of the Father, the Son, and the Holy Spirit. Amen.

Conditioning and Discipline

Do you not know that in a race all the runners run, but only one receives the prize? So run that you may obtain it. Every athlete exercises self-control in all things. They do it to receive a perishable wreath, but we an imperishable. So I do not run aimlessly; I do not box as one beating the air. But I discipline my body and keep it under control, lest after preaching to others I myself should be disqualified. (1 Corinthians 9:24–27)

Blessed is the man who remains steadfast under trial, for when he has stood the test he will receive the crown of life, which God has promised to those who love Him. (James 1:12)

FOR THE COACH

You demand mental toughness, physical stamina, and courage from your student-athletes each and every day. The sprints, agility drills, push-ups, sit-ups, weight training, hill-climbing, repeats, stretching, plyometrics, jump-roping, as well as the relentless energy and focus you require in drills and practices, are for their own good and well-being. An athlete who is in top physical condition has less risk for injury. A player who is focused, disciplined, and mentally tough improves and enhances the gifts God has provided and knows how to properly apply these skills in competition. As team members improve in their sport, so does the overall efficiency and productivity of the team. Well-conditioned and disciplined teams usually experience great success and often defeat more talented, but less disciplined, teams.

Yet, student-athletes often rebel against coaches who demand robust conditioning and discipline efforts. They cheat on their sprints, go through the motions on drills or training runs, or complain that they are not having fun, hoping the coach will shorten practice or offer up a lighthearted game instead of a grueling drill. Fearing disdain or eye rolls from their players, coaches often get intimidated and lessen their own expectations and demands. They start playing music to make practice more fun or come up with other gimmicks to entertain or pamper their student-athletes. They substitute motivational "win one for the Gipper" speeches for blocking and tackling stations. In sport and life, discipline and conditioning get benched in favor of laziness and what makes us happy and comfortable. We take the path of least resistance. This is not to say that you should not mix up your practice schedule a bit or have a fun drill at the end of a practice when your student-athletes really need it. Confident and focused coaches, however, demand excellence no matter how popular or widely accepted the practice plan is among team members.

Of course, even the best conditioned and disciplined teams lose. The same thing is true for our own spiritual lives. No effort on our part will ever get us to heaven or lead us to a sinless life. We will never be in good enough shape to withstand the attacks of Satan. Earthly death cannot be overcome no matter how many vitamins we take or how much we exercise. And we are not disciplined enough to refrain from mistakes, sinful behavior, and our own sinful flesh. This is why God knew we needed a Savior and sent His Son, Jesus, to take away your sins and the sins of the world when He died on the cross.

Disciplined Christians, or disciples of Christ, stay in good spiritual shape by receiving God's Word and Sacrament regularly and faithfully. They get in the Word and stay in the Word. They conduct their own personal devotions or join a regular Bible study. They join a Christian book club. They find a prayer partner. They stay connected to the love of Christ.

Jesus is the *only* program, the *only* one who keeps you in great shape with your heavenly Father for now and for all eternity, so stay spiritually fit as a disciple of Christ. "Just Do It" or, rather, "Just Receive Him."

A DEVOTION FROM THE COACH TO THE ATHLETES

For the moment all discipline seems painful rather than pleasant, but later it yields the peaceful fruit of righteousness to those who have been trained by it. (Hebrews 12:11)

To become a great athlete and a great team, you must be disciplined and in top-notch physical and mental shape. Even when your body says no or your brain says, "I don't want to do this, it's too hard to do right now," I will continue to push you and demand a lot from you. Practice will be much harder than game or competition days so that when you compete against other teams and athletes, you feel prepared and can enjoy the moment and perform at your very best. If I was not disciplining you or asking you for your best each day, that would mean I really did not care about you. God has given you these gifts, and you can glorify Him by using and applying them to the fullest.

God expects a lot from you in your daily walk in life too. He wants you to remain in good spiritual shape as one of His disciples. A lot of people in the world today do not want to follow a God, or higher power, who has "a bunch of rules," as they say. They do not want to be accountable to anyone; they just want to do their own thing. Can you imagine, though, if I let each of you do your own thing on this team? Some of you would take the easy way out. You know you would! Chaos would ensue! We would all be losers. We discipline each other and work hard to stay in shape because we care about one another, the team, and our performance.

God disciplines His children—you and me—and wants us to stay in good spiritual shape because He loves us. The words *discipline* and *disciple* share the same root. He wants us to be His disciplined disciples. He wants the best for us—a close relationship with Him. God did not give us the Ten Commandments because He is a killjoy and does not want us to have any fun in life. He gave them to protect us, show us our sin, and guide our future behavior. God is providing discipline or tough love for His children. His Word is for our spiritual and eternal well-being.

Just like muscles atrophy or get flabby when they are not exercised, your spiritual life and relationship with God will deteriorate if you do not listen to Him or talk to Him. Therefore, receive His gifts of grace in church. Get in and stay in His Word. Listen and talk to Him through devotions and prayer. Let's be the best disciplined and conditioned team in the area this season. More important, let's stay in great spiritual shape as disciples of Christ in our daily walk. We can take comfort in the fact that Jesus, in His perfection, traveled the long and excruciating walk to the cross in our place. What a joy it is to know He continues to walk with us each and every day and keeps us close in His care.

A PRAYER FOR THE ATHLETES

Dear heavenly Father,

Thank You for sending Jesus, Your perfect Son, to pay the price for our sins. He was disciplined enough to go through with Your plan of salvation, brutal as it was. Help us, Lord, to stay in spiritual shape by receiving Your grace in the worship service and through the Word. By the power of the Holy Spirit, inspire us to share Your love and serve as faithful disciples of Christ.

In the name of the Father, the Son, and the Holy Spirit, Amen.

Roll Out the Libero

For You formed my inward parts; You knitted me together in my mother's womb. I praise You, for I am fearfully and wonderfully made. (Psalm 139:13–14)

But God shows His love for us in that while we were still sinners, Christ died for us. (Romans 5:8)

FOR THE COACH

The libero is an essential player on any advanced volleyball team. A defensive specialist and excellent passer who is renowned for keeping the ball in play, the libero has special rules unlike any other player on the volleyball team. For example, you can have only one libero per match, they do not have to rotate around like the other volleyball players do, they cannot play in the front row or attack, they cannot serve, block, or attempt to block, and so on. Plus, the libero usually must wear some cool, different-color jersey. A libero is special.

Like the libero in volleyball, most other sports have their own unique positions that require particular sets of skills and dispositions. A quarterback, a goalie, a linebacker, a midfielder, a lead cross-country runner, a point guard, a pitcher, a shot thrower, a sprinter, a dance-team member, a hurdler, a shortstop—the list could go on and on—possess special skills and a mental makeup that truly differ from other positions on their respective teams. The truth is, to be successful at any of these specialty positions, a player has to have some unique talent, skill, experience, and expertise to execute or perform at a high level. In other words, special positions require special players.

As a Christian coach, God calls on you to recognize the special gifts and talents God has given each of your student-athletes and to encourage them to use them for His purposes. Not every player on your team, of course, has been blessed to be an outside hitter or a libero. In fact, as you well know, some of your players' gifts and talents are not suited for the court or athletics in general. Nevertheless, God placed them on your team and under your leadership and care for a reason. Like a libero knows he or she has a special set of skills and role to play, so, too, does every member of your team. Look for and embrace the specialness of each player.

In the same manner, do not forget that God has given you special gifts, talents, and dispositions. Take the time to reflect on what makes you distinct as a coach. Is it the unusual drills or conditioning you require of your athletes? Is it your personal and tailor-made devotions? Is it the way you meet with your captains each week? Your heartfelt prayers you offer after each practice? The specific verbal and written feedback you give your athletes? Your encouraging, positive attitude? Your intensity? Your approachability? The way you get your student-athletes to improve as the season goes along? Your end of season banquet? Embrace your specialness and make an impact on your athletes in a most compelling manner.

The same holds true in life. You are special, and so are the student-athletes you coach. Remind them that they are all children of their heavenly Father and made in His image. God knew each individual by name before they were born and He even knows the number of hairs on their heads. There are no others like them in the world—there never has been and never will be. Each of your athletes is unique and has been blessed in special ways by God. Most important, Jesus set each of them apart when He shed His blood on the cross for the forgiveness of all of their sins. Jesus' love makes each individual special, even a libero.

A DEVOTION FROM THE COACH TO THE ATHLETES

Having gifts that differ according to the grace given to us, let us use them: if prophecy, in proportion to our faith; if service, in our serving; the one who teaches, in his teaching; the one who exhorts, in his exhortation; the one who contributes, in generosity; the one who leads, with zeal; the one who does acts of mercy, with cheerfulness.
(Romans 12:6–8)

And whatever you do, in word or deed, do everything in the name of the Lord Jesus, giving thanks to God the Father through Him.
(Colossians 3:17)

In volleyball, a libero is a defensive specialist—someone with a particular set of skills and different rules to follow, including wearing a different colored jersey. How special is that!

If you really think about it though, every single position on our team is unique and requires certain abilities and aptitudes. This is true in other sports too. A quarterback has to have a different skill set than a lineman. A hurdler must possess a different kind of talent than someone who throws the shotput. A soccer goalie needs much better hands than does a midfielder or forward. You get the picture. Each position on a team, whether you are a starter or someone who comes off the bench, requires special abilities and a unique outlook and attitude. Put another way, each special position on the team requires a special person or player to fill it.

God put each of you on this team for a reason. Each of you possess different gifts and talents, but all of your God-given abilities and attitudes are needed to make this team the best it can be. Each one of you, no matter how much you play in a game, can contribute to the team's success. And God wants you to use the gifts He has given you—whatever they are—for His purposes and design. He does not desire to see any of His children waste their talents. Instead, He wants you to be a good steward of everything He has given you.

God only made one of you. The Bible asserts that you are "fearfully and wonderfully made" (Psalm 139:14). There has been no one like you in the past, and there will be no one like you in the future. You were made in His image (Genesis 1:27), and God even knows the number of hairs on your head (Luke 12:7). What makes you even more special is that God sent His Son, Jesus, to die for you and take away your sins. You are saved and redeemed.

Until you are called home to heaven someday, do not waste the gifts and talents God has given you. When someone throws away a present you gave them or never uses it, that hurts and disappoints you, doesn't it? Whether your gifts are more evident on or off the court, use them for God's purposes and glory. Be the specialist—the special person—that God made you to be no matter your position or station in life. Lead, serve, and live in His name and for His purposes as He has prepared, in Christ, for you.

A PRAYER FOR THE ATHLETES

Dear heavenly Father,

Often we fail to thank You for all of the blessings we receive, including, most especially, the gift of Your Son, Jesus, who redeemed us from our sins. Strengthen and encourage us to use the gifts and talents You have given us and to serve boldly and joyfully in Your name for Your purposes.

In the name of the Father, the Son, and the Holy Spirit. Amen.

The Big Game or Meet

Peace I leave with you; My peace I give to you. Not as the world gives do I give to you. Let not your hearts be troubled, neither let them be afraid. (John 14:27)

When I am afraid, I put my trust in You. (Psalm 56:3)

So we can confidently say, "The Lord is my helper; I will not fear; what can man do to me?" (Hebrews 13:6)

FOR THE COACH

The boys were tense in the locker room. The bleachers were jammed with fans from the two schools. Standing room only remained. They could hear the pep bands from the two schools blasting songs in an alternating fashion. Cheerleaders were exhorting their fan bases earlier than normal. The sectional final was at hand, and the winning team would advance to the state tournament. Meanwhile, in the locker room, the boys tried to cope with their nervousness.

Realizing his players were especially tight, the coach entered the locker room and directly confronted their anxiety in a light-hearted and intentionally exaggerated way: "Fellas, I've never seen a neutral site packed with so many people," he enthusiastically chirped. "There are probably 10,000 people out there, and *they all came to see you play,*" he emphasized. "Don't mess it up!" He smiled genuinely while embracing the specialness of the moment and knowing his comments would compel a collective and nervous rejoinder. On cue, the guys chided their coach for playing on their anxiety and the pressure they were feeling. Truthfully, however, they treasured their coach's levity and obvious attempt to get them to crack a smile and release their pent-up anxiety.

Usually, coaches do not have to find ways to psychologically prime their players before big games or competitions. If anything, to make sure players are not overly excited or emotionally compromised, coaches sometimes need to bring calmness and a sense of perspective to their teams.

One way Christian coaches can calm the nerves of their players, or get them psychologically prepared, is to remind them that

God put this particular team together for a reason. And like everything God creates and puts His hands to, He saw that it was *very good.* Your team might not be very good in terms of talent or play, but it might be very good in the sense of community, family, and journeying through life's experiences together. Stress the specialness of the moment—that *God* created and put together your team for this particular game. Being nervous before a big game simply means you care and want to perform well. Embrace the pressure. Rejoice and be glad in it!

More important, remind your student-athletes that God has already taken care of the big and important things in life. Salvation and heaven have already been won, thanks to Jesus. This reality should lessen the anxiety and pressure your athletes might be feeling. They might be competing for a conference championship or even a state tournament berth, but they are not fighting tigers and lions in the Roman Colloseum for their very lives. They are playing a game. Knowing that Jesus has done the crucial, life-saving work, your team can play free and loose. After all, what's the worst thing that can happen? Indeed, no matter the outcome of the big game or competition—whether you win or lose (and you want to win!)—nobody can take away the promise and the assurance that Jesus has claimed you and your athletes as His own. He championed each one of you. Spiritually, the team cannot lose, so why not play to win tonight!

In life, your players will face many big challenges, trials, and opportunities. You have the opportunity to teach them to look at life from a Christian worldview. Jesus has taken care of the Most Important Thing, or MIT, in their life—their salvation. Everything else does not seem quite so big or significant from that perspective.

So go for it! Play huge in the big game or competition knowing that your God, and what He did for you, is always bigger than the moment.

A DEVOTION FROM THE COACH TO THE ATHLETES

Do not be anxious about anything, but in everything by prayer and supplication with thanksgiving let your requests be made known to God. And the peace of God, which surpasses all understanding, will guard your hearts and your minds in Christ Jesus. (Philippians 4:6–7)

And God saw everything that He had made, and behold, it was very good. (Genesis 1:31)

I know you all are excited, but maybe a little more nervous than usual, too, about our big game or competition. You know what? I get it. Your nervousness or anxiety means you care and want to do well. I like that. In fact, I would worry about you if you were not nervous or had no anxiety heading into the competition. You are prepared, however, and I know you are going to do the best you can out there. We will be fine.

If I told you that there are approximately 1.5 billion people living in China who don't care that you are playing a game or competing, would I get at least a little smile out of you? Hopefully, it adds some perspective to reality.

Even though you all have worked hard and prepared diligently, we need to remember that this is just a game or competition; it's not life and death. Second, let us not forget that the Most Important Thing (MIT) in our lives has already been taken care of and settled. The big showdown is over. When Jesus died on the cross to redeem you from your sins, His victory over sin, death, and the power of the devil sealed the deal for us. Our salvation is already won. I don't know about you, but if we were competing or playing tonight for whether or not we spend eternity, or the rest of our lives, in heaven or hell, then we would all be justified to be obscenely nervous! Instead, we know that God has taken care of the MIT. As big a game or competition as this is, it's nowhere near as big as what Jesus faced during His crucifixion, so let's play and compete with confidence, poise, looseness, and intensity, knowing that we are already winners and victors in Christ. No one can take that away from us. When it comes to our faith, we literally have nothing to lose tonight, so let's go for it!

Finally, remember that God brought us all here together and for this big game for a reason. Millions of boys and girls around the world will never get a chance to play organized sports, let alone in a big game or competition. Let's embrace the moment and make the most of it. Cherish and enjoy it. Win or lose, His plans for us are always good and grand. May we give Him the glory with our effort and witness.

A PRAYER FOR THE ATHLETES

Dear heavenly Father,

Calm our nerves a bit so that we can focus and play our best with the gifts and talents You have given us. Thank You for giving us the opportunity to compete in a sport we love and for taking care of the really important and essential things in our life: food, clothing, shelter, family, and friends. Most especially, we thank You for the gift of Your Son, who died on the cross and redeemed us from our sins. In Christ is our ultimate victory!

In the name of the Father, the Son, and the Holy Spirit. Amen.

Your PR and a Runner's High

Now on the first day of the week Mary Magdalene came to the tomb early, while it was still dark, and saw that the stone had been taken away from the tomb. So she ran and went to Simon Peter and the other disciple, the one whom Jesus loved, and said to them, "They have taken the Lord out of the tomb, and we do not know where they have laid Him." So Peter went out with the other disciple, and they were going toward the tomb. Both of them were running together, but the other disciple outran Peter and reached the tomb first. (John 20:1–4)

But the one who endures to the end will be saved. (Matthew 24:13)

FOR THE COACH

No matter the place finish in a track or cross-country race, runners generally feel fantastic when they achieve a PR (personal record). One of the beautiful aspects of track and cross-country running is that you not only compete against your opponents, but also against yourself—every day in practice as well as during meets. As a coach, you cannot ask anything more of your runners than to continually improve, thereby lowering their times, and earning PRs. In this way, every one of your runners—from the fastest and strongest to the slowest and weakest—can achieve and win every day.

While PRs are highly desirable in cross-country and track events, there is another PR that is not so good: sin. In fact, your life PR before God is deplorable and deadly. Your selfishness and sin in what you think, say, and do condemn and convict you to death and eternal damnation. Instead of standing on the winner's stage as do victorious cross-country and track athletes, you and all human beings stand on a stage covered and infected by sin and the sinful human condition. Your personal record stinks. And here is the really tough part of this reality: you can do nothing on your own to improve your time or human condition. You cannot get in better shape or shed your sinful nature on your own. You need a Savior.

Graciously and mercifully, your loving, heavenly Father sent His Son, Jesus, to die for you. Your sins are forgiven and have been paid for in full. You can run your life's race with confidence and with a runner's high just like Mary Magdalene, Peter, and John did when they heard the good news of Jesus' resurrection. Jesus has a way of giving people who know Him a runner's high.

Rejoice that your PR before God has been wiped clean and made perfectly pure—more precious than gold or silver, any all-conference medallion, ribbon, or even the satisfaction of a personal best race. While your life's race here on earth will indeed be full of daunting hills and valleys, treacherous potholes and slippery conditions, hampering hot and cold weather, intense cramps, and even debilitating injuries, embrace and celebrate the reality that you are in great shape with Jesus. He will take you through the finish line of life on a runner's high. Thanks to Jesus, your PR never looked so good. By God's grace, keep running strong to the end.

A DEVOTION FROM THE COACH TO THE ATHLETES

I have fought the good fight, I have finished the race, I have kept the faith. (2 Timothy 4:7)

For by you I can run against a troop, and by my God I can leap over a wall. (Psalm 18:29)

Therefore, since we are surrounded by so great a cloud of witnesses, let us also lay aside every weight, and sin which clings so closely, and let us run with endurance the race that is set before us, looking to Jesus, the founder and perfecter of our faith, who for the joy that was set before Him endured the cross, despising the shame, and is seated at the right hand of the throne of God. (Hebrews 12:1–2)

One of the things I love about coaching this sport is how you can compete against yourself everyday—every practice and every meet. Yes, you run and race against other opponents and teams, but the person you race against the most is yourself.

That is why I love it when you achieve a PR in a meet. That should be one of your goals each and every race. You might not be the fastest or the strongest runner in the area, but you can work hard to improve and beat your own times. And really, you should feel joy and a deep sense of satisfaction knowing that all of the training and hard work you put in is paying off and making a difference. If you strive for PRs every day, you can hit the pillow each night feeling good about yourself and using God's gifts to the fullest.

Unlike your race and practice times, however, something none of us can improve upon is our own self-centeredness and sinful nature. No matter how hard we try, we will still think, talk, and act selfishly and sin in thought, word, and deed. That's a life PR that we cannot improve on our own.

Our loving and merciful heavenly Father, though, did not want our PR in this earthly life to qualify us as losers with no hope and lead us to eternal damnation. Instead, He sent His Son, Jesus, to die for you and me and to wash all our sins away. Our PR before God has been wiped clean.

When Mary Magdalene discovered the open tomb on that first Easter Sunday, she *ran* with joy to tell the disciples. When Peter and John heard Mary's testimony, they *ran* back to the empty tomb, even racing each other to see who would arrive first. Jesus does that to people. He gives them life and the ultimate runner's high. When you know the risen Christ, you cannot help but be inspired to jump for joy and live with courage, purpose, and gratitude.

Thanks to Jesus, your PR in life is new, improved, and perfect. He loves you, and someday heaven will be your home with Him. Until you are called home, though, the Bible encourages you to run the race set before you with endurance (Hebrews 12:1–2), to finish the race, to keep the faith (2 Timothy 4:7). By God's grace, run strong every day—on this team and in life with Jesus by your side.

A PRAYER FOR THE ATHLETES

Dear heavenly Father,

Thank You for sending Your Son to die for us so that our personal record of sin would be washed clean and made pure. Inspire us through Your Word to lead and serve, in whatever we do, with a runner's high and the peace and contentment that comes only through a close relationship with You. Help us to be good stewards of all that You have given us, including our athletic abilities. By the power of the Holy Spirit, may we run the race of life with endurance and faithfulness to the end of our earthly days.

In the name of the Father, the Son, and the Holy Spirit. Amen.

urnovers

Many are the afflictions of the righteous, but the Lord delivers him out of them all. (Psalm 34:19)

For at one time you were darkness, but now you are light in the Lord. Walk as children of light. (Ephesians 5:8)

There is therefore now no condemnation for those who are in Christ Jesus. (Romans 8:1)

FOR THE COACH

Turnovers will kill you. In the National Football League, almost every team that makes the playoffs has a positive turnover ratio. Teams that turn the ball over lose possessions and opportunities to score. Moreover, turnovers often provide short fields to score and loads of momentum to the opposing team. Your team can rush and throw the ball for more yards, dominate time of possession, and still lose the game if they turn the ball over too much. Thus, every football coach works hard to instill ball security in his offensive players and a strong aversion to putting the football on the ground or in the opposing team's hands. You install practice drills that emphasize ball security, clean exchanges, check-downs if no one is open downfield, and sound fundamental decision-making. Players receive discipline and punishment for committing turnovers in practice—any psychological or motivational approach is used to help players avoid them in all situations. *And yet*, even though your players know how deadly turnovers can be to the success and efficiency of the team, they still commit them every day in practice and in games. Why cannot these players play the game and refrain from making mistakes like you taught them!

Sin is the killer, the daily turnovers, in our relationship with God. In football, we want to play the perfect game without any errors or mistakes. Yet we fail to do so. The same is true in life. Even though we want to live a perfect life and obey God, our sinful nature and sinful flesh compel us to sin and do the exact opposite of God's desire and commands. Called to put no other gods before the triune God, we put ourselves first and even make ourselves gods—wanting to justify our own desires and actions. We are to love our neighbor as ourselves. Instead, we put our own selfish interests ahead of others and even jealously covet what they possess. Most of us desire to be upstanding Christian leaders—"good guys" and "good gals"—in our daily walk. We know God's Ten Commandments, we know the difference between right and wrong, we know what God expects of us, and yet we use the thoughts, words, and deeds that run counter to His design. We do what is wrong in God's eyes anyway. We rebel and disobey God's Word despite knowing that God only wants what is truly good for us.

Unlike the game of football, where each turnover becomes a part of the permanent record, Jesus erased our sins, our turnovers in life, when He died on the cross and rose again. Jesus gave us victory over sin, death, and the power of the devil. He made us perfect and righteous in God's eyes through the shedding of His blood on the cross.

In football, and in other sports such as basketball, hockey, and soccer, turnovers are often committed because of careless or reckless action, laziness, distractions, a lack of practice and/or confidence, hesitation, confusion, and a failure to understand the scouting report and opponent. In our faith lives, we, too, can allow ourselves to become vulnerable to Satan's temptations and ploys when we are careless and lazy in our church attendance, when we fail to richly and deeply study and meditate on God's Word, and when we neglect to remind ourselves that we are tools and vessels of God and His purposes here on earth. We surely do not want to excuse, accept, or even justify our daily turnovers and sinful way of life. Conversely, when we faithfully and regularly receive God's Word and Sacrament, the Holy Spirit works in our hearts and minds and protects us from Satan's machinations and our own deadly, sinful nature.

The fact remains, however, that we are imperfect human beings living in a fallen world. Nothing we do will eliminate our sin and the turnovers we commit in life. We need our Savior, Jesus Christ, to save us and lead us. Only Jesus can rescue us from our sins and eternal damnation. Only Jesus can make us righteous and perfectly acceptable before His heavenly Father.

The only turnover Jesus ever committed in His life is when He turned Himself over to the Roman guards in the Garden of Gethsemane. That was no sin or mistake, but rather God's merciful plan of salvation unfolding in His perfect time. Jesus' sacrifice on Good Friday was perfect—something we can never be on this side of heaven. Thanks be to Jesus that none of our sins or turnovers in life will ever count against us, and heaven will be our home for all eternity.

A DEVOTION FROM THE COACH TO THE ATHLETES

For I do not understand my own actions. For I do not do what I want, but I do the very thing I hate. Now if I do what I do not want, I agree with the law, that it is good. So now it is no longer I who do it, but sin that dwells within me. For I know that nothing good dwells in me, that is, in my flesh. For I have the desire to do what is right, but not the ability to carry it out. For I do not do the good I want, but the evil I do not want is what I keep on doing. Now if I do what I do not want, it is no longer I who do it, but sin that dwells within me. . . . Wretched man that I am! Who will deliver me from this body of death? Thanks be to God through Jesus Christ our Lord! (Romans 7:15–20, 24–25)

We work so hard in practice and during games to limit our mistakes, to cut down on our turnovers. We constantly practice and emphasize ball security, good decision-making, and the importance of taking care of the football. We even put pressure on each other not to be careless or reckless with the ball. We know that turnovers kill us, and yet we still commit them. As a coach, this drives me nuts!

Such is the way of our daily life too—and I'm sure this must drive our heavenly Father crazy! You see, we know what is right in God's eyes and what pleases Him. We know the Ten Commandments and that God wants us to turn away from our sinful behavior and live a good and God-pleasing life. We know right from wrong, *and yet* we keep on doing wrong and sinning. We want to be faithful Christians and obedient Christian leaders, *and yet* we fall short. This has to drive God crazy just like turnovers do for us on this football team.

Despite our sins and mistakes, He still loves us. He loves us so much that He sent His Son, Jesus, to wash away our sins, our daily turnovers in life, and make us perfect and clean. Only Jesus, who never sinned, could do this. In fact, the only turnover Jesus ever committed is when He turned Himself over to be crucified to pay the price for my sins and yours.

So let us keep striving for clean and error-free football while giving thanks that God's game plan for our salvation was executed to perfection. Thanks be to Jesus.

A PRAYER FOR THE ATHLETES

Dear heavenly Father,

Thank You for sending Jesus to wash away our sins and daily turnovers in life. Help us to fight off the power of the devil and our sinful flesh by hearing and receiving Your Word in church, Bible study, and personal devotions. Through the power of your Holy Spirit, strengthen our hearts and minds and help us to keep our eyes fixed on You.

In the name of the Father, the Son, and the Holy Spirit. Amen.

Homecoming

But according to His promise we are waiting for new heavens and a new earth in which righteousness dwells. (2 Peter 3:13)

For here we have no lasting city, but we seek the city that is to come. (Hebrews 13:14)

But, as it is written, "What no eye has seen, nor ear heard, nor the heart of man imagined, what God has prepared for those who love Him."— these things God has revealed to us through the Spirit. (1 Corinthians 2:9–10)

FOR THE COACH

Whether your student-athletes are in elementary, middle, or high school, Homecoming stirs genuine excitement and anticipation in your school community. In the days leading up to Homecoming Week, students may partake in special dress-up or "spirit days," assemblies, powder-puff football, powder-buff volleyball, dodgeball, class competitions, a school bonfire, cookouts, dances, Homecoming Court elections, pep rallies where teams and players get introduced to the school community, you name it. With the school year still relatively young and fresh and the weather hospitable and temperate, students, parents, and community members alike exhibit great enthusiasm for the annual special event.

As a coach, your task is to channel your student-athletes' extra enthusiasm and keep them focused on the big home meet, match, or game on your schedule that week. After all, the crowds tend to be bigger for Homecoming games. Alumni return. Everyone wants to perform and show their best. Even if you try to persuade your athletes that this particular competition is just like any other during the season, you know the reality: Homecoming athletic contests *are* a little more special, or at least your athletes feel the difference.

As a Christian coach, take advantage of the specialness of Homecoming Week and make it a teachable and memorable event in the faith lives of your student-athletes. During the fall season of athletics, many athletic teams wear pink for a special game or match to bring attention to breast cancer awareness month in October. What would happen if your team took Homecoming Week and did something special with it in regard to witnessing and sharing the love of Jesus Christ—a Jesus Awareness Week, Love Thy Neighbor Week, He Is Risen Awareness Week, or Heaven Is Our Home Week? If your team members want to do something different, take the time to talk about Homecoming Week in advance with your student-athletes and have them come up with a distinctive, spiritual Homecoming theme that testifies to the truth of Scripture, the grace of God, or Jesus' love and sacrifice for all. The general public and community pay more attention to schools and athletic teams during Homecoming Week competitions, so get the athletic department to help with designing and making special T-shirts or accessories for your athletes as well as the fans. Put a Bible verse on them and share the Word of God. Work with the proper school officials to publicize your special theme. Get some enthusiastic parents to help you with these and other Homecoming endeavors and preparations. Whatever you can do to witness and testify the love of Christ, a love that you and your team know and cherish so dearly, do it in championship style. *Make it special and memorable.*

Of course, there will be extra preparation and work required to execute your special Homecoming theme and activities well, but Christian coaches lead and teach in special ways beyond the secular game, match, or competition. Make Homecoming Week not only a special memory, but a life lesson on the eternal. Your athletes, and their parents, will not forget it for the rest of their lives. And that's coaching for life—eternal life.

A DEVOTION FROM THE COACH TO THE ATHLETES

In My Father's house are many rooms. If it were not so, would I have told you that I go to prepare a place for you? (John 14:2)

Go home to your friends and tell them how much the Lord has done for you, and how He has had mercy on you. (Mark 5:19)

Homecoming Week is a special week during the school year, so I am not going to try to pretend that this week's game or competition is not unique in some ways. As your coach, I would be lying if I did not admit that I wonder what your focus will be like in practice and during our competition. I know there are all sorts of fun activities going on that will distract you. So even though I should be trying to get you to focus on the game ahead, there is one more thing—the most important thing—that we need to take time to reflect on during this Homecoming Week. That is, of course, the ultimate homecoming that all believers of Jesus Christ will experience someday. And let me tell you, that will be the greatest homecoming of all time.

The word itself, *homecoming*, is significant. Traditionally, *homecoming* means "a return home"—when alumni come home from college, from the military, or from the work force. The whole community celebrates the return of their favorite sons and daughters.

But the Homecoming you are about to experience this week will not even come close to our eternal homecoming, when we are called home to heaven and sit before the Lamb of God, who took away the sins of the world, including yours and mine. Can you even imagine heaven, a place that is perfect and joy-filled in every way? No more tears, pain, crying, hardship, sin, or difficulties? Can you imagine a place so wonderful that the streets are paved with gold? Most important, heaven is where you will see Jesus, the one who is preparing a place for you in His Father's mansion, the one who willingly and intentionally took the form of a man, died, and rose again so that your sins would be forgiven and so that you could live forever with Him in paradise. This is the eternal homecoming that awaits you, and you do not even have to perform well here on earth or win any match, competition, or game to get there. You are God's homecoming king or homecoming queen. Jesus has taken care of all of that on the cross. You get to enjoy the eternal party and festivities of a heavenly homecoming.

So, this week, amidst all the busyness and Homecoming hoopla, when a large portion of the community is watching us, let us give thanks for what Jesus did for us and share His love. Let us celebrate our school's Homecoming and use it tell people about the ultimate homecoming. Let's make both homecomings special because our Savior is special.

A PRAYER FOR THE ATHLETES

Dear heavenly Father,

During Homecoming, we remember especially the ultimate homecoming that awaits us in heaven, thanks to Jesus. Until we are called home, help and strengthen us so that we might testify to the truth and share the Good News of salvation.

In the name of the Father, the Son, and the Holy Spirit. Amen.

6
WINTER

Preseason Prognostications and Predictions

Therefore the Lord Himself will give you a sign. Behold, the virgin shall conceive and bear a son, and shall call His name Immanuel. (Isaiah 7:14)

For to us a child is born, to us a son is given; and the government shall be upon His shoulder, and His name shall be called Wonderful Counselor, Mighty God, Everlasting Father, Prince of Peace. (Isaiah 9:6)

FOR THE COACH

Several decades ago, when his Georgia Tech Yellow Jackets were ranked #1 in the NCAA preseason polls, Coach Bobby Cremins was asked what he thought of the flattering forecast. Instead of deflecting the high praise of his program, as many other coaches would certainly have done, he embraced the acclaim: "I love it," the coach said. "Pressure makes diamonds."

Most coaches, however, do not like discussing preseason predictions. After all, a highly ranked or regarded team should win and produce great results. If the team does well, people expected those results. On the other hand, a lowly ranked or regarded team faces the temptation of allowing the preseason prognostication to become a self-fulfilling prophecy. The team might not have the opportunity to shape its own identity, or perhaps the fan base simply assumes that there is nothing worth watching or seeing. Preseason rankings and prognostications, however, are part of the landscape in the sports world. Even the smallest elementary school team has preseason expectations and buzz, positive or negative, amongst fans and school constituents.

Christian coaches look at forecasts with a biblical worldview. You understand that God assembled your team for this time and for His purposes. And He *chose you* to teach and lead these precious student-athletes.

So, to coin a phrase, just do it! Lead, teach, and embrace the specialness of your team. You will never have another one like it. Remind your players that preseason predictions are often wrong, incomplete, and inadequate. Flawed human beings, as we all are, often make erroneous predictions.

In contrast to the imperfect sporting prognostication over the years, the Bible's numerous prophecies and predictions about the coming Messiah were 100-percent accurate. Hundreds of years before Jesus was born in a little stable in Bethlehem, Old Testament prophets predicted His birth, mission, death, resurrection, and so much more about His life. As the prophet Isaiah wrote, "Behold, the virgin shall conceive and bear a son, and shall call His name Immanuel" (Isaiah 7:14). This Savior, Jesus, would be "pierced for our transgressions;" He would be "crushed for our iniquities;" in Him we would receive "peace," because through "His wounds we are healed" (Isaiah 53:5). God's plan of salvation unfolded exactly as predicted.

Immanuel means "God with us." Sometimes preseason rankings, especially if the expectations are high, do cause high anxiety or stress as players and coaches feel pressure to perform and meet expectations. As a Christian coach, however, remember that God is with you and your team. Remind yourself, and your team members, that God designed and assembled your team "for such a time as this" (Esther 4:14). He has a plan and a purpose for bringing your team together, though you may not see this clearly at all times.

Knowing that God is always present and with you should lessen the pressure and alleviate anxiety. God created you and your team, and He will not abandon you, no matter what happens during the season. Moreover, God has different expectations and plans for your team than the so-called experts and fan base do. So, while you exhort your players to strive for excellence, conference championships, and rivalry game victories, remind your team to "do everything in the name of the Lord Jesus, giving thanks to God the Father through Him" (Colossians 3:17). You coach and they play for victories, but also for the *One*. We do this because we know Jesus ranked each of us #1 when He died on the cross to take away our sins. This act of sacrificial love, accompanied by His resurrection from the dead on Easter Sunday, redeemed us forever from the power of sin, Satan, and our sinful flesh. We will finish #1 in heaven because of our Savior, Jesus Christ.

The Bible was "written so that you may believe that Jesus is the Christ, the Son of God, and that by believing you may have life in His name" (John 20:31). If you want to make any preseason predictions, try this one: Our team will give honor, praise, and glory to You this season, dear heavenly Father, because Your Son redeemed us and made us #1.

A DEVOTION FROM THE COACH TO THE ATHLETES

Rejoice greatly, O daughter of Zion! Shout aloud, O daughter of Jerusalem! Behold, your king is coming to you; righteous and having salvation is He, humble and mounted on a donkey, on a colt, the foal of a donkey. (Zechariah 9:9)

But He was pierced for our transgressions; He was crushed for our iniquities; upon Him was the chastisement that brought us peace, and with His wounds we are healed. (Isaiah 53:5)

The start of the season is upon on us. We are still growing as a team, trying to figure out who we are and how good we can become together. Many have already made up their mind or predicted what kind of team we are going to be and what kind of season we will have, before we even play one game.

In our world, predictions and forecasts often fail to come true. Whether it be tomorrow's weather, the Super Bowl champion, or the next president of the United States, many human predictions are, quite frankly, unpredictable and unreliable. Many predictions simply do not come true.

Conversely, the accuracy and fulfillments of the predictions and prophecies made in the Bible in regard to Jesus Christ are stunningly and amazingly precise. Numerous biblical prophecies, many written hundreds of years before the coming of Christ, did come true and were fulfilled by Jesus. After the fall of Adam and Eve, God promised a Savior. And He delivered on that promise by sending His innocent Son into this world.

Knowing how much He loves us and "that for those who love God all things work together for good, for those who are called according to His purpose" (Romans 8:28), let us be mindful that God brought this team together. God assembled this team, and He is with us each and every day. His presence gives us great comfort and inspires us to play and give all honor and glory to our heavenly Father.

So here is one prediction that has already been proven true: God's love for you will never change or waver. God is the *one* who put you #1 in His loving plan of redemption from the very beginning of time. God predicted and promised a Savior after the fall of Adam and Eve, and He delivered. Jesus came. He died and rose again. He fulfilled and validated Scripture's predictions and prophecies. God sure does know how to pick 'em and predict 'em.

A PRAYER FOR THE ATHLETES

Dear heavenly Father,

Thank You for being reliable and dependable, and for fulfilling the prophecies by sending Jesus to redeem us from our sins. You took Your one and only Son and made each of us #1 by cleansing us from our sins. We give thanks that we can cling to and count on Your Holy Word yesterday, today, and tomorrow.

In the name of the Father, the Son, and the Holy Spirit. Amen.

Backboard or Rim?

Do not be unequally yoked with unbelievers. For what partnership has righteousness with lawlessness? Or what fellowship has light with darkness? . . . Or what portion does a believer share with an unbeliever? What agreement has the temple of God with idols? For we are the temple of God with idols? For we are the temple of the living God; as God said, "I will make My dwelling among them and walk among them, and I will be their God, and they shall be My people. Therefore go out from their midst, and be separate from them, says the Lord, and touch no unclean thing; then I will welcome you, and I will be a father to you, and you shall be sons and daughters to Me, says the Lord Almighty." (2 Corinthians 6:14–18)

FOR THE COACH

Do you tell your players to use the backboard or shoot straight at the rim? One thing is for certain: If players keep varying the technique—one time using the backboard and another time aiming straight at the rim—they will never develop the consistent approach necessary to become a good shooter and scorer. Indecision and fickleness hinder proficiency and excellence.

There are a lot of different ways to find success in basketball. Zone, man-to-man, full-court, half-court, and junk defenses have all been philosophies and approaches employed by championship programs. Teams that play up-tempo or walk the ball up the court have also won consistently. Some coaches holler and shout at their players; others use few words and calmness to get their message across. Some coaches like to schedule tough non-conference opponents, while others like an easier schedule to build player confidence. Some teams use nine or ten players for regular game action; others rely primarily on their starting five for major playing time. The point is that while there are many different ways to approach the game, coaches must be clear about their vision and expectations. Players need to know exactly what the coach expects of them and what kind of team they are striving to be. You cannot teach and motivate one way on Monday, and then coach and lead a completely different way on Tuesday—not if you want to build trust and confidence. If your coaching philosophy lacks conviction, commitment, and certainty, if you only work at it half-heartedly, you will lose the respect and clarity necessary to lead the team, and deservedly so.

The Bible teaches that God despises it when Christians are "lukewarm" or indifferent to the faith. Too many followers of Christ are convenient Christians—they look, talk, and act like Christians when it is easy and safe to be that way, but abandon or deny the faith when confronted with ridicule, persecution, or derision. They present themselves as strong, outspoken Christians on Sunday, but they talk and behave like pagans on Friday and Saturday nights. Or they say, "I'm with you God," one day and ignore or deny Him the next.

Just like a basketball coach who wants his players to be totally committed to the team and program—both during the season as well as during the off-season—God wants your heart (Proverbs 23:26) and total dedication. No outstanding or self-respecting coach would ever accept and allow athletes to display apathetic or lazy attitudes in practice. Nor does God. Scripture says God will spit us out of His mouth (Revelation 3:16)—His loving care—if we act like fair-weather Christians.

One important reason God does not want us to be lukewarm toward Him is that Satan is scheming for our souls and preys on those who are weak, indifferent, or lukewarm about their relationship with Christ. God does not want to lose you, or any of your student-athletes, to Satan. He sent His one and only Son to die on the cross to pay for your sins. God's plan of salvation was decisive, intentional, and clear. There was nothing convenient or lukewarm about it.

As a Christian coach, care for your players' souls as much as you do for their execution on an out-of-bounds play. Remind them of the very real competition we each have with sin, our sinful flesh, and the power of devil. The Good News is that while we cannot win the battle or contest for our souls on our own, Christ has already given us the victory.

So teach your players to shoot for either the backboard or directly at the rim. Just be intentional and decisive—the same way Jesus went to the cross for you. Indeed, there was nothing lukewarm about Christ's blood and love for you.

A DEVOTION FROM THE COACH TO THE ATHLETES

I know your works: you are neither cold nor hot. Would that you were either cold or hot! So, because you are lukewarm, and neither hot nor cold, I will spit you out of My mouth. (Revelation 3:15–16)

For any athlete and team, being clear and decisive are important. If you hesitate or do not commit to something, bad results usually occur. Take, for example, those midrange jump shots. You have to decide if you are going to use the backboard or shoot directly at the basket or rim. If one time you aim for the backboard and the next time directly at the rim, you will not be an accurate or consistent shooter or scorer from that range. Same thing on the defensive side of the ball: If you trap the ball handler on the baseline one possession but not the next, the defensive rotations will unravel, resulting in confusion, uncertainty, and frustration for the entire defensive unit. The same is true in life. You cannot blow an uncertain trumpet and make beautiful music. You do not tell someone you love them, and then treat them with spite and hate.

The Bible clearly explains that God does not want us to be indecisive, lukewarm Christians. Do you like it when someone is your friend one day but treats you like dirt the next? Well God does not want people to conveniently love and obey Him on Sunday but then reject and ignore Him on Monday. God wants your complete devotion and heart all of the time. As sinners, of course, we know that we disappoint Him with our sins in thought, word, and deed.

Thank God, however, that He sent Jesus to redeem us. He was not indecisive or hesitant in rescuing us from the eternal damnation we deserved. Instead, God sacrificed His one and only innocent Son for all of humankind, and for *you* too. And He wants a special, meaningful, ongoing relationship with you. He loves you that much.

So make up your mind what you are going to aim for: the backboard or the rim. More important, remember that God wants you all in on your relationship with Him—nothing lukewarm or halfway. After all, His Son, Jesus, went all in for you on the cross. His love for you is clear, decisive, and everlasting. Since Jesus is better than any backboard or rim, keep your eyes fixed on Him today and always.

A PRAYER FOR THE ATHLETES

Dear heavenly Father,

Forgive us when we demonstrate a lukewarm faith and devotion to You. Remind us that You definitively and decisively acted on Your plan of salvation, through Your Son, to redeem us. By the power of the Holy Spirit, may we clearly and confidently be salt and light in this world so that others might know the love and forgiveness of Jesus Christ.

In the name of the Father, the Son, and the Holy Spirit. Amen.

Where's the BEEF?

Set your minds on things that are above, not on things that are on earth. (Colossians 3:2)

FOR THE COACH

Even the youngest of basketball campers learn the fundamentals of shooting through the acronym BEEF (balance, eyes, elbow, and follow-through). A good shooter, no matter what level of play, demonstrates proficiency in all four attributes. Thus, coaches constantly remind players to form a *balanced* base with their feet, focus their *eyes* on the rim, keep their *elbow* tucked-in or behind the ball, "reach into the cookie jar," and *follow through* consistently. Usually, if a shooter goes into a slump, one or more of these fundamentals are out of whack.

Next time you remind your players about BEEF in shooting or free throw drills, take the time after practice, or before your next practice, to talk about BEEF from a faith perspective. Indeed, too many people in our world today lead *unbalanced* lives. Consumed with worldly things and temptations, they focus on themselves and their sinful desires instead of keeping their *eyes* on God's Word and *everyone else's* needs. Soon, like that elbow that pops out during a shot, they discover their life priorities are all out of alignment *everywhere* and wonder how they ended up in such disarray. Or they may have good intentions—"I'll try to get to church this Sunday"—only to *fail in following through* with their promise or resolution. As a busy basketball coach, you may find living a balanced life is challenging with work, basketball, and family all competing for your precious time and attention. Divorce rates are high among coaches because many fail to keep their eyes focused on the health of their marriage or follow through by attending to their spouse's needs.

In the biblical account, Peter, while walking on the water, took his eyes off Jesus. At that very moment, he was distracted by the wind and he sank. It is the same with you and your players. When you do not keep your eyes fixed on Jesus, when your life becomes unbalanced and you crowd out time with God in church or Bible study, you sink in your sins and risk drowning in your own sinful ways and sinful nature. Your players do too.

Many coaches lead off the year proudly and piously telling parents, players, and administration that God comes first, family second, schoolwork third, and then basketball. Then the season begins, and reality fails to match the rhetoric.

As a Christian coach, you have a powerful platform and position to model and promote God-pleasing practices and priorities in life. Just like a good basketball team requires sound fundamentals to be taught, practiced, and encouraged, Christians need reminders and encouragement to live their faith and recognize what is most important in life, namely their relationship with Christ. If you are failing to live out your faith-inspired priorities, you are not alone. Just like He did for Peter, Jesus picks us up when we fail and fall.

Ask God to help you BEEF up your program's and team's fundamentals in regard to everyone's relationship with Jesus. Remind your players to live a *balanced* life and to keep basketball in proper perspective. Encourage and show them how to keep their *eyes fixed on Jesus* and God's Word. *Follow through* with the faith-development activities you have prioritized and established as a team. Giving a team devotion and making faith applications each and every night/day is a great start to creating a BEEFed-up program.

Would it not be sad if the season ended and your players wondered, "Hey coach, where was the BEEF?" In a culture that values the sizzle more than the steak, give them the Savior who triumphed over sin. That is a delectable main course with the best (heaven) yet to come.

A DEVOTION FROM THE COACH TO THE ATHLETES

Therefore, since we are surrounded by so great a cloud of witnesses, let us also lay aside every weight, and sin which clings so closely, and let us run with endurance the race that is set before us, looking to Jesus, the founder and perfecter of our faith, who for the joy that was set before Him endured the cross, despising the shame, and is seated at the right hand of the throne of God. (Hebrews 12:1–2)

Many years ago, Wendy's put out a commercial with a cute little senior citizen complaining that other fast-food restaurants hardly put any meat in their burgers. The little old lady came back up to the counter of these competitor establishments, pointedly asking the question: "Where's the beef?" The tagline became legendary.

I am not sure if basketball coaches borrowed from this popular commercial or not, but in shooting a basketball, many coaches, including those in our program, teach you to be fundamentally sound using the acronym BEEF. To be a good shooter, you need to get your feet set with a sound base or good *balance*, keep your *eyes* attuned to the rim, align your *elbow* properly with your legs and shoulders, and *follow through* with your wrist and shooting hand. These fundamentals are important to learn and master, and that is why we practice them daily.

If we change the meaning of the letters in the acronym BEEF just a bit, they also provide a good way for us to remember the priorities of our spiritual lives. God wants us to live a *balanced* life. As much as we love it, basketball, or any entertainment, can become our god if we let it. When God said in His Word that "You shall have no other gods before Me" (Exodus 20:3), He knew the human tendency to get our priorities mixed up and out of balance. The Bible also tells us to keep our *eyes* fixed on Jesus—the founder and perfecter of our faith—and the *eternal life* that only He can provide (John 3:16). Often, we get easily distracted with so many other things and ignore the time we should spend with God in prayer, Bible study, and personal devotions. Finally, inspired by the Holy Spirit, we remain *faithful* and receive God's Word and Sacraments in regular, faithful church attendance.

As important as it is to work on BEEF fundamentals in basketball, it is even more important to encourage one another, so that we may we never ask "Where's the BEEF?" in terms of our faith walk with God.

A PRAYER FOR THE ATHLETES

Dear heavenly Father,

Thank You for making each of us Your priority when You sent Your one and only Son, Jesus, to die on the cross and take away our sins. Inspired by Your love, may we live a balanced life, fix our eyes on Jesus and Your Word, bask in Your promise of eternal life, and faithfully and regularly worship and receive Your grace in Your house of worship.

In the name of the Father, the Son, and the Holy Spirit. Amen.

Sharing the Rock

Do nothing from selfish ambition or conceit, but in humility count others more significant than yourselves. (Philippians 2:3)

Each one must give as he has decided in his heart, not reluctantly or under compulsion, for God loves a cheerful giver. (2 Corinthians 9:7)

Oh come, let us sing to the LORD; let us make a joyful noise to the rock of our salvation! (Psalm 95:1)

FOR THE COACH

Ball hog, ball stopper, black hole, hardwood pounder, "his next pass will be his first"—these are labels and phrases that no coach or student-athlete says with affection about another player. Indeed, no one likes to coach or play with a selfish player. Because no matter how talented, selfish players ultimately hurt the team or, at the very least, keep the team from becoming as good as it could be. In the same manner, selfish human beings, no matter how successful they first might appear, eventually reap the fruits of their sinful labors. They drain people and kill joy, energy, trust, and enthusiasm. They are takers, not givers. On the other hand, everyone loves to coach or play with a teammate who is self-effacing, unselfish, humble, and focused on the needs of others. Coaches treasure leaders who make teammates better, put the needs of the team ahead of their own, and encourage peers when they need a pick-me-up.

In the game of basketball, when someone makes a pass that directly leads to a score, the player registers an assist. Assists rarely garner the publicity that scoring does, but successful coaches know that players who create and provide easy scoring opportunities for others are invaluable. Exemplary coaches specifically and publicly praise players who "share the rock" or do other unselfish and blue-collar work (e.g., screening, rebounding, playing tough defense, getting loose balls, etc.). Many even create their own special recognition and reward systems, highlighting statistics and achievements other than points scored.

You can go even deeper to encourage selflessness in your players by pointing to Jesus and God's Word. "Love your neighbor as yourself," Jesus tells us (Mark 12:31). Moreover, the Bible asserts that we are to "count others more significant" than ourselves (Philippians 2:3) and to be "cheerful" givers (2 Corinthians 9:7). These commandments and exhortations of God refer to all vocations of our lives, including basketball. Therefore, Christian basketball players lead, compete, and play unselfishly and cheerfully. They encourage one another. They put the needs of others ahead of their own and count others as more important or significant than themselves.

God shared His one and only Son with us despite our sinfulness and selfishness. Indeed, while we were still selfish and sinful, Christ died for us (Romans 5:8). Talk about an assist or putting you in position to score in life now and forever. Jesus delivered you from the clutches of Satan, hell, and your own sinful flesh. His unselfish act—His big-time assist—gave you salvation. God gave up the Rock for you.

Give thanks that your God is a generous and merciful God. He literally shared Jesus—the Rock of your salvation (Psalm 95:1)—with and for you. He thought of you before His own Son.

God calls you, inspired by His sacrifice, to be a cheerful giver, to shout Jesus' name from the bench, and to share the Good News from your coaching platform. God enlisted you to nurture and encourage your players' faith walks and to put their spiritual needs at the top of your priority list. If you can teach your players to share the Rock—the Rock of our salvation—watch the Holy Spirit take over and bless your student-athletes on and off the court. Grab some popcorn. You will have the best seat in the house.

A DEVOTION FROM THE COACH TO THE ATHLETES

Go therefore and make disciples of all nations, baptizing them in the name of the Father and of the Son and of the Holy Spirit, teaching them to observe all that I have commanded you. And behold, I am with you always, to the end of the age. (Matthew 28:19–20)

Therefore encourage one another and build one another up, just as you are doing. (1 Thessalonians 5:11)

In any team sport, we know it takes a team effort to be the best team we can be. No one likes playing with a selfish player, someone who is more interested in his own statistics, his own points, his own way, or his own publicity rather than the team's goals and objectives. Selfish players suck the life out of a team, poison a positive atmosphere, turn off team unity, terminate trust, and dampen enthusiasm. If you are going to be a member of this team, you have to put the team first and your own individual needs and desires second.

One of the reasons I love to see a player dive on the floor for a loose ball, screen a defender, take a charge, play tough defense, or share the rock is because I love seeing players who are unselfish and get the big picture. This team is not about just you. Of course, you are part of it. In fact, each one of you is a critical part of our team. But this team, just like life, is not all about you. The Bible says that we must "encourage one another and build one another up" (1 Thessalonians 5:11), and "do not neglect to do good and to share what you have, for such sacrifices are pleasing to God" (Hebrews 13:16). Encouraging, building, sharing, sacrificing, giving—these are characteristics of Christian leaders not just on a basketball team but also in life.

Since we are sinful human beings, we often act selfishly. We do not treat others—including our family, loved ones, teammates, and friends—as we would like to be treated ourselves. This is certainly not how God commands us to treat others. We even put ourselves ahead of and before God. We want to become gods.

The good news for you and me is that Jesus put your needs first and His needs second. God knew we would need a Savior to redeem us from our sins. Enter Jesus, the Rock of our salvation. Yes, you heard it right, God shared the Rock—His beloved and innocent Son—so that you and I might score eternal salvation in heaven.

During this season and beyond, my prayer for all of you is to never turnover or lose the Rock—the Rock of our salvation. Instead, may the Holy Spirit give you a big-time assist when you share the Rock with others.

A PRAYER FOR THE ATHLETES

Dear heavenly Father,

Even though we did not deserve Your mercy and grace, we thank You for sending Your Son, Jesus, who gave His life for us so that we might live forever in heaven. Inspired by the forgiveness of sins and Christ's love, help us share the Rock of our salvation and spread the Good News to others.

In the name of the Father, the Son, and the Holy Spirit. Amen.

The Lead Guard

A new commandment I give to you, that you love one another: just as I have loved you, you also are to love one another. By this all people will know that you are My disciples, if you have love for one another. (John 13:34–35)

And let us not grow weary of doing good, for in due season we will reap, if we do not give up. So then, as we have opportunity, let us do good to everyone, and especially to those who are of the household of faith. (Galatians 6:9–10)

FOR THE COACH

Every basketball coach craves a super lead guard, the player who will handle the ball against pressure, initiate the offense, settle the team down when under duress, and win a game in multi-dimensional ways: scoring, passing, rebounding, and defending. Even more important, a coach desires a lead guard who is the team's preeminent leader, the one who puts the needs and wants of others before himself or herself and demonstrates tenacity, fearlessness, sacrifice, teamwork, and unselfishness. If you have one of these lead guards, give thanks to God for this blessing. And if you do not yet have a true lead guard, start molding, shaping, and encouraging one of your players to *become* that kind of player and leader. You will not only have a better team because of your efforts, but you will be teaching this individual key leadership skills that will serve him or her well in life to come.

Our world needs Christian leaders—lead guards in life—more than ever. Way beyond the game of basketball or any sport, you are teaching and nurturing young people to become Christian servant leaders in a world full of evil, corruption, emptiness, and loneliness. As Christians, we know the love of Christ and what He did for us on the cross. This is why we care for and serve others in Jesus' name. The Holy Spirit compels and inspires us to love our neighbor as ourselves and to reach out in love as Christ first did and continues to do for us. Most important, we serve others so that we can share God's Word and Christ's love in all its truth and purity. If faith comes by hearing the Word of God, we can and should use basketball as a platform to share Scripture with one another as well as with the school community.

If you truly care about someone, you are going to share Jesus with this individual. If you truly care about your players, you are going to share Jesus and God's Word with them. And if your players truly care for their teammates and friends, they are going to share Jesus with those friends too.

As a coach, you can be like that unselfish lead guard you hope to have leading your team. Remind your players to stay on point, focusing on Jesus and the forgiveness of sins that only comes through Him. By God's grace and as an instrument of His love, you can distribute the Rock—the Rock of our salvation—to your players every day.

A DEVOTION FROM THE COACH TO THE ATHLETES

Let each of you look not only to his own interests, but also to the interests of others. (Philippians 2:4)

Therefore encourage one another and build one another up, just as you are doing. (1 Thessalonians 5:11)

With the Crusaders down two points with only seconds remaining in the game, Josh took an outlet pass and raced down the court looking to score. Suddenly, three defenders closed on him to stop the ball and guard against an attempted three-point shot. Streaking down the court on the opposite side was his teammate Danny. Josh faked a three-point attempt and then threw a beautifully placed bounce pass to Danny, who had cut to the basket with no other defender around him. With the clock set to expire, Danny went up for the layup—and missed the shot as the buzzer sounded! Danny would normally hit this shot ninety-nine times out of a hundred, but not tonight. Immediately, he put both hands on his head and began to sob. As the players shook hands and headed to their respective locker rooms, Danny remained inconsolable even as his teammates tried to comfort him. After the team had showered and dressed, Josh approached Danny: "It was my fault, Danny," the senior point guard insisted. "The pass could have been a little bit better." The truth is that the pass had been as close to perfect as you could make under the game conditions and circumstances, but Josh wanted to find a way to alleviate some of Danny's despair. He was thinking of his teammate's needs and feelings before his own. When some other players told the coach what Josh had said and done, the coach simply responded, "That's just the kind of kid and leader Josh is."

Josh put Danny's feelings and interests ahead of his own. He took the blame for the missed layup so that his teammate could move on and not be burdened by his failure. That is what Christian servant leaders do—they think of others first and put others first. That's what unselfish basketball players or student-athletes do too—they put their team and their teammates ahead of their own desires and wants.

Our Lord and Savior, Jesus Christ, of course, is the best example in history of putting the needs of others ahead of Himself. Think about it: He did nothing wrong. He lived a perfect life. And yet, in addition to the spitting, beatings, scourging, and nails He endured, Jesus took on all of our sins, and the sins of the entire world, and washed them away when He shed His blood on the cross. He took the blame and responsibility, not for a missed basket at the end of a game, but for our sins and sinful flesh. He put our greatest needs—forgiveness and redemption—ahead of His own. He gave His life for us. Now that is pure unselfishness.

Because of Jesus' perfect sacrifice, our lives will not end with an earthly buzzer. We will not come up one basket short of paradise. Our lives will not end in a permanent loss. Instead, our lives will be laid up in heaven someday. Heaven is our home. Victory is ours in Christ. Redeemed, we praise and give thanks to Jesus now and forever.

A PRAYER FOR THE ATHLETES

Dear heavenly Father,

We know it is very easy to think only about ourselves—our own needs and concerns, how our lives are going, or how well we are playing our sport. Forgive us, heavenly Father, for our own selfishness—our own sinful thoughts, words, and deeds. Help us to look to You and think about others instead of ourselves. Help us to see the hurts, pains, and needs of those with whom we come in contact. Encourage us to use the gifts You have given us to notice, reach out, and help those around us in a God-pleasing manner. Inspire us to give a beautiful testimony to share the love You show us daily through the death and resurrection of Your Son, Jesus.

In the name of the Father, the Son, and the Holy Spirit. Amen.

Rebounding

In this you rejoice, though now for a little while, if necessary, you have been grieved by various trials, so that the tested genuineness of your faith—more precious than gold that perishes though it is tested by fire—may be found to result in praise and glory and honor at the revelation of Jesus Christ. (1 Peter 1:6-7)

So we do not lose heart. Though our outer self is wasting away, our inner self is being renewed day by day. For this light momentary affliction is preparing for us an eternal weight of glory beyond all comparison, as we look not to the things that are seen but to the things that are unseen. For the things that are seen are transient, but the things that are unseen are eternal. (2 Corinthians 4:16-18)

FOR THE COACH

Teams that rebound usually win . . . a lot. If defense (almost always) wins championships, then rebounding is an essential skill and component of basketball. Rebounding is the last thing a team must successfully execute before they convert from defense to offense. In other words, the final element of good defense is a rebound!

Coaches treasure players who love to rebound and do it well. Most local newspapers keep track of the leading conference scorers but not the leading rebounders. Rebounding is not flashy. Sometimes called the "dirty work," rebounding is about attitude, determination, want-to, technique, and hard work. Moreover, terrific rebounders are students of the game—they notice shot trajectories and understand how and where missed shots will carom so they can seize favorable rebounding positions on the court.

When a team gets a rebound, the game instantly turns or reverses course. Players sprint to the other side of the court. After a rebound, your team is now dictating the game on offense, where you have the opportunity to score. Rebounding literally changes the direction and flow of the game.

Such is true in the life of a Christian too. Nowhere in the Bible does God tell us that the life of a Christian will be easy. Sin, suffering, pain, disappointment, disillusionment, death—these all permeate our fallen world and each of our lives. In other words, all of us will experience setbacks, tough times, and tragedies.

Coaches tell their players to "block out" their opponent in order to retrieve the basketball on a rebound. Yet we know that we cannot block out our sins, mistakes, or the selfishness and evil that exists in the world. In a fallen and decaying world, it is not a matter of *if* bad stuff will happen but *when*. And when bad stuff happens, the real question is this: can *you* rebound?

The truth is we cannot rebound on our own when it comes to our spiritual lives. We cannot overcome our sinful nature with our own works or achieve salvation on our own. Coaches teach their players "to put a body on someone and block out" when they rebound. In order to rebound from life's trials and setbacks, we have to get in the proper position too: on our knees confessing and repenting of our sins as we also seek God's grace and guidance. We also must make contact, not with the opponent's body, but with our Savior. Christians know that when they fall, sin, or experience hardship, Jesus is right beside them, ready to offer help and hope. Jesus will pick us up and help us rebound in life. Even in the valley of hardship, the Good Shepherd will not let us be forgotten nor forsaken.

Teach your players the art of rebounding in life. Encourage them to seek out Jesus and His Word during their trials, temptations, and life's valley moments. Remind them that Jesus rebounded from His crucifixion splendidly on Easter Sunday. Our Savior specializes in comebacks, resurrections, second chances, and new life. No matter how hard you fall or crash, Jesus will pick you up, help you finish the race, and give you the peace that surpasses all human understanding.

A DEVOTION FROM THE COACH TO THE ATHLETES

Count it all joy, my brothers, when you meet trials of various kinds, for you know that the testing of your faith produces steadfastness. And let steadfastness have its full effect, that you may be perfect and complete, lacking in nothing. (James 1:2–4)

God is our refuge and strength, a very present help in trouble. (Psalm 46:1)

[Cast] all your anxieties on Him, because He cares for you. (1 Peter 5:7)

We know that one key ingredient of playing great defense is to end the possession with a rebound. When we grab a rebound, we get a defensive stop, and now we can transition to offense and score. That is why I love rebounders. I love players who do the little things or the dirty work to help us be successful. Your name probably will not get in the newspaper or sports blogs for rebounds, but winners and winning teams rebound!

Rebounding is essential in the life of a Christian too. You have probably heard the phrase or wondered, "Why do bad things happen to good people?" Maybe something bad or terrible happened to a member in your family, to a close friend, or to you. The truth is this sinful and fallen world is full of heartbreak, pain, suffering, and hardship. I know each of you has experienced setbacks, made mistakes, or had bad things happen in your life. Too many people, unfortunately, try to rebound from life's setbacks and adversity by relying only on themselves.

There is no "I" in "rebound," however, when it comes to real life and all things eternal.

In regard to your faith life, the only one who can help you rebound from your sinful nature and eternal damnation is Jesus Christ. When He died on the cross, He took away all of your sins. He made an incredible defensive stop on your path toward eternal damnation. Because of Jesus, you are heading to heaven on a divine fast break.

In addition to the redemption and life rebound you have in Christ, Jesus remains a safe, most loving outlet for you. When you experience setbacks, hardship, or tough losses in life, do not try to rebound from every challenge or handle these moments or issues by yourself. Go to Jesus. Place your worries, burdens, tribulations, and concerns into the hands of your loving Savior. He will repair your heart, fill your emptiness, and bring peace and joy to your soul. With Jesus doing all the work, you will rebound—in this life and the next.

A PRAYER FOR THE ATHLETES

Dear heavenly Father,

Help us to rebound from setbacks, pain, suffering, hardship, and tough times. When we do something wrong and sin, forgive us. When someone or something hurts us, comfort and uplift us. Most important, thank You for sending Your Son, Jesus, who saved us from our sins and provided the ultimate life rebound for us.

In the name of the Father, the Son, and the Holy Spirit. Amen.

The MIT (Most Important Thing) on the Court

For by grace you have been saved through faith. And this is not your own doing; it is the gift of God. (Ephesians 2:8)

He has delivered us from the domain of darkness and transferred us to the kingdom of His beloved Son, in whom we have redemption, the forgiveness of sins. (Colossians 1:13–14)

For this is the will of My Father, that everyone who looks on the Son and believes in Him should have eternal life, and I will raise him up on the last day. (John 6:40)

FOR THE COACH

"Everybody just stop! Stop where you are right now!" the coach yelled at his players. "What is the most important thing (MIT) on the court?" The players looked at one another sheepishly because they knew Coach was upset at their porous defense. "What is THE most important thing on the court?" he yelled again. "You, Coach?" one player half-kiddingly and half-seriously answered. "Nice try. It's not the worst answer I've ever heard," the coach retorted, half-amused and half-irritated. "The MIT on the court is the ball! They can't score without the basketball! It doesn't matter if you have your person guarded or covered like a blanket if the ball somehow goes through the hoop. Stop the ball! It's the MIT on the court!" To be a good defensive team, players must be able to locate and stop the MIT on the basketball court.

The MIT of Christianity is not about how kind and compassionate you are, how many good works you can do for your neighbor, or how many service projects or charitable endeavors you participate in within your community—though these are all wonderful ways to show the love of Christ. For the Christian, the MIT is knowing Jesus Christ as Lord and Savior, the one who died on the cross to save you from your sins.

As Jesus is the MIT in your life and the lives of your players, make sure you dedicate quantity and quality time to this most important relationship. Coach up your kids on the importance of finding and stopping the basketball on defense, but then remind them daily of the MIT in life: Jesus' sacrifice and unconditional love for them. Lead your team in devotions and Bible study. Monitor your players' church attendance, and encourage them to the worship service faithfully and regularly. If they do not have a church home, invite them to your home congregation. Ask your captains and other team leaders to take their turn leading Bible study and team devotions. The point is, if an intimate relationship with Jesus is the MIT in life, you and your players need to listen to Jesus, talk to Him, teach about Him, and live in Him. Make the MIT the highest priority on your daily coaching agenda. Rejoice in knowing that Jesus made you the Most Important Thing when He went to the cross on your behalf.

A DEVOTION FROM THE COACH TO THE ATHLETES

Jesus said to her, "I am the resurrection and the life. Whoever believes in Me, though he die, yet shall he live, and everyone who lives and believes in Me shall never die." (John 11:25–26)

Jesus said to him, "I am the way, and the truth, and the life. No one comes to the Father except through Me." (John 14:6)

To be a good defensive team, we have to concentrate on finding and stopping the basketball on defense. The ball is the most important thing, the MIT, on the court. The only way you can score points in this game is if that little round ball goes through the hoop. If we keep the ball from going through the basket, the other team cannot score. Ball pressure, help-side defense, taking a charge, help and recover, sinking to the level of the ball, deflections, good rebounding position, getting a hand in the passing lanes—none of these sound defensive skills or techniques can be executed without knowing where the MIT is on the court.

The MIT on the basketball court, however, is nothing compared to the MIT in your daily life—and that is, of course, your relationship with Jesus Christ. He was God's plan for our salvation from the very beginning of time. Trapped in our sin and sinful flesh, God so loved the world and so loved you that He sent His one and only Son to rescue us from our sins. *You* were that important to Him. His mercy, grace, and love for you are that profound.

Too often in games or practice, we lose sight of the ball, and our defense breaks down. The other team scores an easy basket because we forget, lose, or get careless with the MIT. We cannot do that if we want to be a great defensive team. We have to find and see the ball.

Likewise, let us encourage one another to make sure we never lose sight of the MIT in our daily faith walk. When we ignore His Word and skip church, we take our eyes off the prize, the MIT in our lives. Giving up two or three points to our opponent in a basketball game is bad enough, but to give up, ignore, or take our eyes off Jesus, well that is a tragedy of epic and eternal proportions.

So, when you are on the court, find the ball and stop it! When you step off the court and merge back on the road of life, remember to locate and listen to Jesus, your Savior and Best Friend. By God's grace, keep the MIT the MIT in your life now and forevermore.

A PRAYER FOR THE ATHLETES

Dear heavenly Father,

Often, we fail to put no other gods before You or to make You the most important thing, the top priority in our lives. By the power of the Holy Spirit, strengthen our faith and our relationship with You. Help us to encourage one another in our church attendance, Bible reading, and personal devotions so that we may hear Your Word and grow closer to You. What a privilege it is to carry everything to You in prayer—our joys, thanksgivings, and burdens. You are our Savior, and this truth gives us comfort and confidence to live each day with purpose as directed and inspired by You. Thank You for loving us and watching over us each and every day.

In the name of the Father, the Son, and the Holy Spirit. Amen.

Killer Penetration

If anyone teaches a different doctrine and does not agree with the sound words of our Lord Jesus Christ and the teaching that accords with godliness, he is puffed up with conceit and understands nothing.
(1 Timothy 6:3–4)

FOR THE COACH

There is nothing that stresses a basketball team or makes its defense more vulnerable to breakdowns than killer penetration. Killer penetration creates easy baskets for the opponent and usually gets your team in foul trouble. Thus, most coaches teach the importance of keeping the opponent out of the lane, or middle of the floor, and keeping yourself between them and the basket. Other coaches emphasize cutting off dribble penetration along the baseline. Either way, an opponent's penetration creates havoc and is certainly lethal to your team's defensive efficiency.

There are other temptations and challenges that can be lethal to a team's success too. Laziness, gossip, premarital sex, jealousy, selfishness, arrogance, a lack of trust—these are killers to team harmony and togetherness. When players know about other players' indiscretions—underage drinking, academic fraud, bullying, theft, fights over girlfriends or boyfriends, just to name a few— and nothing is done to confront and rectify these situations, dissension reigns and team unity suffers. Players lose respect for coaches who are either oblivious to these developments or, worse, know about the indiscretions and do nothing to address them. This is killer penetration of a different sort.

As a Christian coach, be attuned to your players' spiritual well-being, trustworthiness, and relationships. Proactively talk about the temptations they face at home, at school, and on social media. Lead and model God-pleasing behavior. Encourage your players to lean on God's Word and go to God in prayer. Talk about Matthew 18 and how Christians, if they feel they are being wronged by someone, have a biblical obligation to share their grievance privately with that individual first. When you sin, confess it and apologize. Ask for your players' forgiveness in addition to God's forgiveness. When you sense friction or distrust among your players, work with your captains to get the issues out in the open. Do not let problems fester and become bigger predicaments down the road.

As bad as killer penetration is on the court, Satan's killer penetration is even more deadly. Employing lies, distortions, and twisted half-truths, the devil lives to pull people away from Christ and to get them to doubt the inerrancy and truth of God's Word. Perhaps these lies sound familiar:

◎ God did not really create the world; a big bang exploded, the world gradually came into existence, and some primordial soup started cooking.

◎ Babies in the womb are not really people; therefore, protect and defend a woman's reproductive rights.

◎ Jesus welcomed all to the table; therefore, you should accept alternative lifestyles too.

◎ Jesus was not really divine; He was a dedicated public servant and social justice advocate.

◎ Attending church is not really necessary. You can worship God on the golf course, on a lake, or at a community fun run.

◎ Humans are not born sinful; everyone has good in them.

◎ Christ did not have to die for your sins; you can get to heaven by doing many good works in your community.

◎ There are many different religions and paths of enlightenment that lead to paradise or salvation. Choose the one that is best for you.

Unfortunately, Satan's killer penetration has become accepted mainstream ideology in our world today.

Roman crucifixion relied upon killer penetration too. The nails that went through the hands and feet of Jesus, along with the asphyxiation, killed Him on Good Friday more than two thousand years ago. But Jesus was different than the other thieves and criminals executed in such a brutal way on a cross. For He rose, just three days later, completing God's plan of salvation and saving us from our sins. Sin, death, and Satan were defeated one time for all time.

To stop killer penetration on the court, most defenders rely on help from teammates and fundamentally sound team defense. Christians, of course, rely on Jesus Christ, crucified and triumphant, God's Word, and the power of the Holy Spirit to stop Satan's lies, temptations, and attacks on our faith.

Therefore, reinforce good Christian defense with your players. Encourage faithful church attendance, an active prayer life, and daily Scripture and devotional reading. Walk the talk in your own faith life. Talk about temptations your players face when the basketballs stop bouncing. God has given you a special platform to care for your players' spiritual well-being. By God's grace, teach them how to rely on God and His Word to repel killer penetration.

A DEVOTION FROM THE COACH TO THE ATHLETES

For the time is coming when people will not endure sound teaching, but having itching ears they will accumulate for themselves teachers to suit their own passions, and will turn away from listening to the truth and wander off into myths. (2 Timothy 4:3–4)

As a basketball team, we know how important it is to stop the ball and keep the opposing team from driving and getting into the lane. We work hard to stop penetration and keep our defense from breaking down and providing easy scoring opportunities for our opponent. To be successful on defense, we have to stop killer penetration.

We also need to be on guard against a killer penetration of a different sort—this one even more lethal and important than anything that might happen on a basketball court. Things that keep us away from receiving God's grace and mercy in church, that makes us doubt the truth of God's Word, and that stokes up "sexual immorality, impurity, sensuality, idolatry, sorcery, enmity, strife, jealousy, fits of anger, rivalries, dissensions, divisions, envy, drunkenness, orgies, and things like these" (Galatians 5:19–21) are signs that the devil and our sinful flesh are penetrating too deep and killing us inside. Unfortunately, since we are sinners, we have to admit that we do indeed break down and cannot stop this killer penetration on our own.

Knowing we would need a strong defense against our own sinful nature and the devil, God sent His Son into the world for us, for *you*. When the nails penetrated Jesus' hands and feet and He was crucified, your sins were forgiven. The cosmic contest was over. Victory was, and is, yours. Nothing will ever penetrate or break down the cross and the love Christ has for you.

A PRAYER FOR THE ATHLETES

Dear heavenly Father,

Thank You for sending Your Son—our Rock and our Shield—to redeem us from our sins. Until we are called home, help us to encourage one another in our church attendance, Bible reading, and prayer life so that we may remain well-defended from our sinful flesh and Satan's killer penetrations.

In the name of the Father, the Son, and the Holy Spirit. Amen.

Ankle Taping

One who is faithful in a very little is also faithful in much, and one who is dishonest in a very little is also dishonest in much. (Luke 16:10)

He said to them, "Because of your little faith. For truly, I say to you, if you have faith like a grain of mustard seed, you will say to this mountain, 'Move from here to there,' and it will move, and nothing will be impossible for you." (Matthew 17:20)

FOR THE COACH

Many people watch basketball coaches on television or in the movies and presume that coaching is simply some kind of exercise in demonstrating guts and reveling in glory a la *Hoosiers*. Hollywood would have you believe that a great coach simply gives a terrific motivational speech, draws up a picket fence play, and wins a state championship. The coaching gig does not seem all that daunting.

As you are more than aware, coaches spend a considerable amount of time doing grunt and behind-the-scenes work, such as ankle taping, which is not very glorified or desirable. Yet without proper ankle taping, your players would not be able to practice or play during the season. Ankle taping is important.

Often in our faith walk, we fail to attend to the crucial and necessary ankle taping of our soul. We neglect personal Bible study and devotions—the one-on-one time with our God. Instead of preparing our hearts and minds for worship, we stay up late on Saturday night (well into Sunday morning) and barely keep awake in the pew, or we simply hit the snooze button all the way through the worship service, never leaving our bed. We fail to read devotions to our children during the rare supper times when the entire family is together or before going to bed for the night. We forget to take everything to our Lord in prayer.

Great teams pay attention to the details and all aspects of the program, including individual improvement. In the same manner, exemplary coaches operate at a high level in all aspects of the program and not just on game day in front of a big crowd. Taping ankles and taking care of the little details separate the great programs from the good programs.

As a Christian coach, pay attention to the details, the behind-the-scene faith development of your players. They may be wearing a mask and pretending to have their faith life all together while really feeling empty, alone, or lost. They do not want to let you see their hurt or reality. After all, you are a Christian coach, coaching Christian players. They are supposed to have their faith life and religious act together.

That is why it is important for you to check on your players' faith maintenance, that they are receiving and studying God's Word and living in that grace so that their lives do not run aground or go down the wrong path. Daily, proactive spiritual care can nurture a soul for the long haul, just like taking care of an ankle can keep a player on the floor and in the game.

So tape those ankles with dutiful joy. Sweat the details of your program. Most important, in regard to your players' spiritual walk (and yours), encourage them to be faithful in the little things. You can tape their ankles, but only God can mend and strengthen their souls.

A DEVOTION FROM THE COACH TO THE ATHLETES

All Scripture is breathed out by God and profitable for teaching, for reproof, for correction, and for training in righteousness, that the man of God may be complete, equipped for every good work.
(2 Timothy 3:16–17)

Simon Peter answered him, "Lord, to whom shall we go? You have the words of eternal life." (John 6:68)

It was 8:55 a.m. on a Saturday morning when two young assistant coaches arrived at the gym. They promptly went out onto the gym floor to supervise the players who were already warming up. Standing out in the middle of the floor talking hoops and mentally patting themselves on the back for being early, they looked around for the head coach, who was nowhere in sight. Thank goodness they had arrived before the 9:00 a.m. practice had begun so that at least one coach was present to supervise these athletes. At 8:59 a.m., two more players appeared on the court, their ankles taped, soon followed by the head coach. Expecting a thank-you for providing official supervision in the gym, the two assistant coaches were shocked and became suddenly deflated when the head coach gruffly said, "I want to talk to you two guys after practice." The two-hour practice went fine, but the meeting between the three coaches afterward did not. "I need you two to be here at least forty-five minutes before practice to do all the little things coaches need to do," the head coach stated emphatically.

"Like what?" one of the younger assistants responded.

"Things like taping players' ankles before practice!" he asserted. "There is a lot more to coaching than showing up and running drills. You need to learn how to tape ankles."

There is a lot more to coaching than simply running drills during practice and deciding what defense and offense to run during games. The same holds true for being a player on a team. There are so many behind-the-scene things that most of your friends, parents, classmates, and fans would never know or see that make our team go. People do not see the hard work most of you put in during the offseason, the weight-training, stretching, conditioning, and all the early or late practices you endure. They do not see you ice and heat your injuries, the sacrifices you make, and the time you spend away from family and friends. They do not know about the conflicts, drama, and mental fatigue you all endure throughout the season. On the other hand, they do not get to witness the laughter, the bonding, the bus rides, the special team meals, the unique conversations, or our team meetings and devotions. They do not see the ankle taping either. All they see is your play during games. Doing the little things today can make a big difference tomorrow.

In our daily faith walk too, we know that what may seem like little moments of proactive behind-the-scenes soul maintenance— taking time for daily devotions, Bible reading, and prayer—are actually significant and crucial to one's faith and relationship with God. When you talk to God through prayer and listen and receive His life-saving and life-changing Word, the Holy Spirit strengthens and increases your faith. Just as a good tape job protects your gimpy ankle, taking the time to talk and listen to God helps you grow in your relationship with Him and protects you from sin, death, and the power of the devil.

Let us keep doing the little behind-the-scenes things to help us be the best basketball team and players we can be, ankles included. More important, and by God's grace, may you be inspired to receive God's Word daily so that your souls may be well in Christ.

A PRAYER FOR THE ATHLETES

Dear heavenly Father,

While we can work hard to nurture and take care of our bodies, even taping our ankles to limit or lower the odds of a sprain or injury, only You and Your Word can cleanse us from our sins and protect us from sin, death, and the power of the devil. Thank You for healing, strengthening, and protecting our souls, both today and forever.

In the name of the Father, the Son, and the Holy Spirit. Amen.

There Is No "I" in "Team" but There Is in "Win"

He must increase, but I must decrease. (John 3:30)

For everyone who has been born of God overcomes the world. And this is the victory that has overcome the world—our faith. Who is it that overcomes the world except the one who believes that Jesus is the Son of God? (1 John 5:4–5)

FOR THE COACH

Assistant head coach Tex Winter once told all-time NBA great and legend Michael Jordan that there was "no 'i' in 'team.'" To which the ultra-competitive Jordan responded without hesitation, "But there is an 'i' in 'win.'"

Coaches want to win. Even when winning might not be the highest priority, depending on the age-level of the players or reality of the situation, coaches would rather win than lose.

You would like to believe that winning is important to your players too. And probably, for many of your players, winning is important . . . or is it? Ask yourself these questions: Do the players who often sit on the bench for most of the game really care about winning? Would they be okay with losing if it meant they would play more minutes? Would your "star" players rather average twenty points a game on a losing team or average five points a game on a winning team? Many kids today play in weekend tournaments and might play as many as four games a day. They win some and lose some, but tomorrow they might play another four games. Do they really care that much about winning? What exactly does "winning" mean to players today?

The truth is that in our postmodern, YouTube, instant-gratification, it's-all-about-me culture, players most often put their own desires first and then think about their teammates and winning on the scoreboard second. For many, "winning" is about looking good and feeling good about one's own performance. If the team also happens to win the game, that is simply frosting on the cake.

To be sure, one indicator of a winning culture is when players recognize that they are part of a team, something much bigger than themselves. Starters sympathize with those who play few or no minutes in game after game but are expected to practice, participate, and cheerlead with enthusiasm and intensity. Role players earnestly support the starters when they come to the bench during timeouts or when they need a positive word of encouragement during a shooting slump or highly contested game. Winning cultures and teams do not worry about who scores the most points, plays the most minutes, or gets the most credit. Winners think of others and the team first, and themselves second.

John the Baptist, among other things, was a respected religious leader and attraction, baptizing hundreds of people in the Jordan River every day back in his time. Yet, when he saw Jesus, he said, "He must increase, but I must decrease" (John 3:30). As important as John the Baptist's ministry was, he knew that there was only one Son of God and that only Jesus could take away the sins of the world, and yours too.

While John 3:30 rightly points out the essential point that Jesus should be the priority and center of our lives, the verse also encourages coaches and players to decrease their own self-centeredness and to increase their attention and concern for others. Ask yourself these questions: How can I lift up my student-athletes, serve them, and put their needs above my own? How can I make my teammates better and feel like an integral part of the team?

As a Christian coach, remind your athletes that they *are already* winners in Christ. Therefore, in every aspect of their lives, including the platform they have in basketball, your players have the opportunity to glorify God and give a testimony of His love. When people walk into the gym during a game, they should easily recognize and identify the team that puts others first, plays unselfishly, uses their God-given talents to the fullest, competes with passion, and expresses gratitude in all circumstances, even when things go bad.

God is not concerned about who wins or loses a basketball game, but He does care about losers. Indeed, He came for all sinners who were destined for damnation and transformed us into undeserving winners through His death and resurrection. There is no "i" in "Jesus," but there is an "us." Jesus won eternal salvation for us. He sacrificed Himself for you and your players. He put your needs and the needs of others ahead of His own. That's servant leadership. That's winning over sin, death, and the power of the devil. That's our Savior.

A DEVOTION FROM THE COACH TO THE ATHLETES

Do nothing from selfish ambition or conceit, but in humility count others more significant than yourselves. (Philippians 2:3)

It is not good to eat much honey, nor is it glorious to seek one's own glory. (Proverbs 25:27)

The Bible tells us that we must decrease and Jesus must increase in our lives. This is hard to do, isn't it? Personally, I often think, talk, and do selfish things and sin in thought, word, and deed. We all often think of ourselves first, maybe others second, and often we even forget to think of God at all.

Speaking of increasing and decreasing, what if we increased our concern and service to others and decreased our own self-centeredness and selfish thoughts and behaviors? What if, on this basketball team, we constantly thought of our teammates and their needs first and ourselves and our needs second?

There is an old saying that there is no "i" in the word *team*, but there is an "i" in the word *win*. To have a winning team and culture at anything, not just basketball, however, you have to have members or players who put the needs of others ahead of their own wants and needs. In other words, winning teams are packed with unselfish players.

Jesus put the needs of others—namely yours—above His own. He was perfect in every way and lived a sinless life, yet He willingly endured a horrific death on the cross to wipe away your sins as well as the sins of all people. You were redeemed and made special. Heaven is your home and the eternal victory is yours in Christ.

Inspired by His love and sacrifice and by the Holy Spirit, let us be more Christ-like on this team, at home, in school, and in life in general. Live in JOY: put Jesus first, Others second, and Yourself third.

A PRAYER FOR THE ATHLETES

Dear heavenly Father,

We know that we will often sin, fail, or come up short of our goal or objective. Help us to respond to these setbacks with resiliency, gratitude for the lessons learned, and determination to make the best of all situations. May our setbacks and losses in life remind us of our own inadequacies and imperfections and how much we need You as our Savior. You need to be number one in our lives. And since we know of our own sinful nature and shortfalls, help us to be more forgiving of others and to put their needs above our own. You are not only our Savior but the Savior of all. Thank You for Your victory over sin, Satan, and our sinful flesh. May we be salt and light and give a good testimony of Your love to all people.

In the name of the Father, the Son, and the Holy Spirit. Amen.

The Christmas Party

So, whether you eat or drink, or whatever you do, do all to the glory of God. (1 Corinthians 10:31)

These things I have spoken to you, that my joy may be in you, and that your joy may be full. (John 15:11)

And the Word became flesh and dwelt among us, and we have seen His glory, glory as of the only Son from the Father, full of grace and truth. (John 1:14)

FOR THE COACH

Whether you are coaching older or younger student-athletes, young men or young women, girls or boys, Christian coaches give Christmas parties for their players. Just do it. You will never regret it.

The winter sports season is a long season, and you demand a lot of your players. They know their *coach* well. Your players, however, also need to see the non-coach side of you, the complete you—your family life, home, and love for the Lord. You also need to see your players in something other than a uniform or practice jersey. You need to see them as the special kids or young adults they are. If you have not been throwing Christmas parties for your teams, start doing so this season. You and your players have a terrific reason to celebrate the season, both the basketball season and, of course, the season of Advent and Christmas.

Put together a party at your house or at a local restaurant with a meeting room. Invite parents to join you to ensure proper supervision. Break out some games or activities that fit the personality of your team well. Serve up delicious food and baked goods. Give your players a personalized, meaningful gift or keepsake (it does not have to be expensive). Write each of them a special note in a card. Exchange white elephant gifts. Take a team selfie in hideous Christmas sweaters. Laugh with one another. Sing carols. Go Christmas caroling in the neighborhood. Let the players tell jokes. Get together in a circle and toss a popcorn ball around. Whoever catches the popcorn ball has to say one thing he or she most appreciates in another teammate and then pass the ball on to someone else. Watch a short, humorous video. Tell each one of your players, in front of the group, what a treasure and gift he or she is to you, personally. Most important, before they leave the party, read a Scripture passage about the birth of Christ. Have a team prayer where the players take turns giving thanks to God for something special in their lives. Tell them what Christmas means to you and why you are so glad they are a part of your life.

Hosting a Christmas party for your players just might be the best coaching decision you make all season. The babe of Bethlehem came into the world to redeem you and your players for eternity. Be a different kind of coach and get your team together to celebrate the greatest birthday and victory of all time.

A CHRISTMAS DEVOTION FROM THE COACH TO THE ATHLETES

For to us a child is born, to us a son is given; and the government shall be upon His shoulder, and His name shall be called Wonderful Counselor, Mighty God, Everlasting Father, Prince of Peace. (Isaiah 9:6)

"For unto you is born this day in the city of David a Savior, who is Christ the Lord. And this will be a sign for you: you will find a baby wrapped in swaddling cloths and lying in a manger." And suddenly there was with the angel a multitude of the heavenly host praising God and saying, "Glory to God in the highest, and on earth peace among those with whom He is pleased!" (Luke 2:11–14)

Hey, thanks for coming over tonight. I just wanted to say a few words to you, and then we can get back to our eating, games, and partying. You are all busy people, and I'm excited to have you over to my house, not just to celebrate our basketball or sports season, but also to take time to celebrate the Advent and Christmas seasons.

I do not know what is on your Christmas wish list or what gifts you hope to get for Christmas this year, but I want you all to know that Christmas came early for me. Each of you is one of God's special gifts to me. I know I do not always act like it or treat you like the special gift from God that you all are. I know I sometimes frustrate each of you, even disappoint you. Nevertheless, I want you to know how honored and privileged I am to coach you and have you be a part of this team. No matter how much you play or how well you perform on the court, God made each one of you special and put each one of you on this team for a reason. I give thanks and praise to God for that.

Teams go through a lot together—good times and bad times. Teams should also give thanks and celebrate together. Tonight is not just a Christmas party but a birthday celebration. We gather as a team in fellowship to celebrate the birth of Jesus more than two thousand years ago. You see, while we were still sinners, God sent His perfect and innocent Son into the world to save us from our sins. He sent His Son, the babe of Bethlehem, into the world for us. He was called Immanuel, which means "God with us." This was God's plan of salvation, and it is the greatest gift you and I could ever receive.

You have seen me get excited when we play great defense, execute on offense, or have an incredible come-from-behind win. Nothing, however, gives me greater joy than knowing that each of you knows Jesus and what He has done for you. Nothing is more important either. I do not always take the time to tell you this, but I really wanted you to hear that message tonight. Whatever sport you play, it will have an ending someday. Every season comes to an end. Even your playing days will come to an end. God's love for you, however, will never end.

So Merry Christmas to you each of you. And if you do not mind, help me wish Jesus a happy birthday . . . on three now, okay? *One, two, three . . .*

A CHRISTMAS PRAYER FOR THE ATHLETES

Dear heavenly Father,

As we prepare for the coming of the Christ child during this Advent season, help us be mindful of the reason for the season and the true specialness of Christmas. You loved us so much that You were willing to send Your Son into the world to redeem us from our sins. By God's grace, may we be inspired to share the babe of Bethlehem and the Christmas story with our neighbors and friends. To you, O Lord, do we give all praise, honor, and glory.

In the name of the Father, the Son, and the Holy Spirit, Amen.

Timeouts

For where two or three are gathered in My name, there am I among them. (Matthew 18:20)

And let us consider how to stir up one another to love and good works, not neglecting to meet together, as is the habit of some, but encouraging one another, and all the more as you see the Day drawing near. (Hebrews 10:24–25)

And they devoted themselves to the apostles' teaching and the fellowship, to the breaking of bread and the prayers. (Acts 2:42)

FOR THE COACH

In the early 1990s, Fab Five member Chris Webber of the Michigan Wolverines called timeout at a crucial moment at the end of the national championship game against North Carolina. The problem was his team did not have any timeouts left. After assessing a technical foul and losing possession at this critical juncture in the game, the Wolverines lost the championship. Knowing how to use timeouts is paramount to coaches and players.

In the game of basketball, each coach or team receives a limited number of timeouts. Some coaches love to conserve them for specific situations at the end of the game. Others like to use them to stop the momentum of the game, to teach, to give their players a timely rest, or to draw up a crucial must-have play. Almost all coaches, however, cherish their timeouts because they offer opportunities to refocus and direct players to prioritize what is most important at a particular moment in a game. When players get reckless, careless, undisciplined, frustrated, or overwhelmed, timeouts are often beneficial because they can change the momentum of the game.

In the hustle and bustle of life in this fallen world, timeouts are crucial and essential to a Christian's faith walk and spiritual wellness. Indeed, one way Satan loves to subtly and slowly pull a Christian away from God is to keep him or her busy and distracted from what is most important in life. Satan plants many distractions in order to get Christ-followers to skip church and ignore Bible study time, for he knows we need to confess our sins, hear the good news of salvation, and receive God's grace and mercy anew. If Jesus is our Best Friend and Savior, we need to take time to listen to His Word and pray to Him. Any close relationship involves substantive, two-way communication.

As Christians, however, we often fail to take timeouts from our earthly pursuits and self-centeredness. Fishing, golfing, boating, shopping, family vacations, coffee shop time, youth sports, to name a few examples, often slowly but subtly erode worship time on Sundays or weekends. Boyfriends, girlfriends, parties, sports, homework, sleep, social media—anything and everything—become a priority ahead of a growing relationship with Christ. Soon the momentum of life has one trying to overcome the world on human merit and effort. Reliance upon one's self increases, while dependence and trust in Jesus and God's Word decreases. As the saying goes, if you wake up one morning and feel a long way from God, guess who moved?

As a coach, you will develop your own philosophy on how, why, and when to use your timeouts. For the spiritual good of your team, however, insist that your players take daily timeouts to listen to God's Word and talk to Him through prayer. Encourage them to remember the Sabbath Day and keep it holy (Exodus 20:8). Model and walk the talk in these areas of life yourself. Remind your players that everyone is a sinner and needs to receive God's grace and mercy daily and in the worship service. These spiritual timeouts—faithful worship, daily Bible reading, unceasing prayer—not only change the momentum in one's earthly life, but also provide spiritual sustenance for our eternal life.

The truth is that we do not know when our time here on earth will run out, so call spiritual timeouts regularly and abundantly. Huddle up. Take out your Bible. Draw up the cross and empty tomb. Get refocused on Jesus. Then get back out there . . . and coach and live for Him.

A DEVOTION FROM THE COACH TO THE ATHLETES

So faith comes from hearing, and hearing through the word of Christ.
(Romans 10:17)

Pray without ceasing. (1 Thessalonians 5:17)

Let the word of Christ dwell in you richly, teaching and admonishing one
another in all wisdom, singing psalms and hymns and spiritual songs,
with thankfulness in your hearts to God. (Colossians 3:16)

You all know I generally don't like to call or take timeouts during a game when I haven't planned them. I do not want to admit weakness as a coach or team. When I do call a timeout, however, and we huddle up, I usually have something important to say and not a lot of time to say it. I try to use timeouts to stop the momentum if things are not going our way, to get you to refocus on fundamentals that will make us successful, to draw your attention to something really critical in the game, to discipline you, to encourage you, or to draw up some play at a crucial juncture in the game. Sometimes the game is just going too fast, too helter-skelter that you don't even realize what is happening out there. These same reasons for timeouts on the basketball court apply to our daily faith walk and life too.

I don't know if you have thought about this before, but you only get thirty or forty-five seconds to say something in a timeout—something that is really important. So let me talk to you in this timeout of life.

Don't let your life get so helter-skelter and busy that you forget to be still and know that He is God. The play you should draw up each week is to get to church where you can listen and receive God's Holy Word. Make it a regular and fundamental habit to read your Bible faithfully and regularly. When life's momentum is going *well* for you, come to church and God with a grateful and humble heart. When life's momentum is going *badly* for you, come to church and God with a grateful and humble heart. Recognize and worship Jesus as your Lord and Savior, the only one who died on the cross for you and forgives you all your sins. Let God's Word discipline and encourage you.

In the game of basketball, timeouts are optional and may not even be necessary. Sometimes timeouts do indicate a weakness or that an adjustment must be made. In the game of life, however, regular and divine timeouts remain essential because we *are* weak and vulnerable without Jesus in our daily lives. Just like a basketball game, life moves by fast. You can easily get distracted by other shiny, much less important things, so take a daily time-out and read God's Word. Take a weekly timeout and receive His grace in the worship service. You will come out of these timeouts renewed, focused, humbled, thankful, forgiven, and overjoyed. You can never have or take too many spiritual timeouts.

A PRAYER FOR THE ATHLETES

Dear heavenly Father,

In our daily lives, we take timeouts to be refreshed in Your love and forgiveness. We pray that Your Holy Spirit may strengthen us to always trust and call upon You—in good times and bad. In the midst of our busy lives, help us focus and rely upon these spiritual timeouts—church attendance, prayer, and Bible study—seriously and faithfully, for we want to grow closer to You.

In the name of the Father, the Son, and the Holy Spirit. Amen.

Making and Filling Buckets

You prepare a table before me in the presence of my enemies; You anoint my head with oil; my cup overflows. (Psalm 23:5)

The steadfast love of the LORD never ceases; His mercies never come to an end; they are new every morning; great is Your faithfulness. (Lamentations 3:22–23)

FOR THE COACH

Great basketball teams make lots of buckets. Great coaches fill lots of buckets—their players' psychological buckets. Great Christian coaches share Scripture and let the Holy Spirit fill their student-athletes' spiritual buckets. So how are you doing at filling buckets?

All players need encouragement. Athletes who practice hard day after day but rarely play in games need to know you recognize and appreciate their effort. Your star players, who seldom seem to get flustered or make mistakes, want your reassurance and confidence, especially after an uncharacteristically poor performance. Managers, statisticians, and other volunteers crave acknowledgement for their essential behind-the-scenes contributions. Assistant coaches desire to know their time and insights are valued. Indeed, every person associated with your team or program wants to be valued and needs daily encouragement and affirmation.

Too often well-intentioned coaches forget to fill their players' buckets even as they relentlessly teach the *x*'s and *o*'s of the game. Drills and schemes are important to work on, of course, but so is the practice of encouragement. As a coach, you are either uplifting or discouraging your student-athletes (sometimes by silence or indifference). Never forget that your student-athletes are not robots but emotional human beings who need Christian love, affirmation, tenderness, and a kindhearted word from their coach whom they admire and respect greatly. Many athletes scrutinize and wrestle with their own failures or shortcomings more harshly than you ever would as their coach. Even players who do not visibly demonstrate their frustration, sadness, or dejection need encouragement.

Invest heavily in filling your players' buckets. This is a funda-mental aspect of coaching that often separates the great coaches from the good coaches. Encouraging and nurturing your players' mental psyche builds their confidence. Confident, well-grounded players are better mentally prepared to receive your constructive criticism and coaching in a positive manner.

The Bible exhorts Christians to be encouragers, to build one other up in the Body of Christ. You have lived longer and under-stand the ways of our fallen world, but your young student-ath-letes are just beginning to comprehend how cold, cruel, heartless, selfish, and depressing this world can be. Ugliness and negativity confront them every day. You see it. Your players feel it.

Thus, in a discouraging world that empties people's buckets, nurture and fill your student-athletes' buckets with God-pleas-ing encouragement. Praise and affirm their stewardship, effort, teamwork, resilience, courage, determination to learn and grow, and the ability to recover from failure and mistakes. Do not let them get away with poor body language and negative self-talk. Initiate communication and contact with each player after a tough practice or game. Check in with them even if you have not noticed anything unusual. Identify and praise their specific God-given gifts and attributes, basketball and otherwise. Send an affirming text or give a handwritten note of encouragement. Thank your players individually for being an important part of your life.

Most important, cut through this dark world with the light and love of Jesus Christ. Inspire your student-athletes with God's love and promises. Share God's Word and let the everlasting power of the Holy Spirit work on their hearts and minds. Let their bucket, or cup, overflow with God's grace and mercy (Psalm 23:5).

In basketball, a basket made counts as two or three points and might contribute to a victory on the court. But a bucket filled by the Holy Spirit builds and inspires faith and leads to a special re-lationship with the Lamb of God and an eternal reunion in heaven. Train your players how to fill buckets on the court and teach them to let the Holy Spirit fill their spiritual buckets for life. Score big-time on and off the court for today and for eternity.

A DEVOTION FROM THE COACH TO THE ATHLETES

Gracious words are like a honeycomb, sweetness to the soul and health to the body. (Proverbs 16:24)

There is one whose rash words are like sword thrusts, but the tongue of the wise brings healing. (Proverbs 12:18)

How many points do we get when we score a basket or bucket? Correct! Two or three points, depending on the distance. And just in case anyone is wondering, I am in favor of scoring and making lots of buckets! As long as there is scorekeeping, I would rather score more points and make more buckets than the opposing team.

In addition to filling some buckets on the court, we can fill each other's personal buckets too. Be on the lookout for ways you can encourage, praise, and lift up your teammates. For instance, have you thought about how hard it is to come to practice each day and go through the same drills and practice schedule but not play as much during the game? How might you show appreciation and fill the buckets of your teammates who work just as hard as you do but do not get to play as much? How might you fill the bucket of a teammate who is really down because of a bad game or because of a personal issue?

In addition to filling the buckets of your teammates, you have an opportunity to fill the buckets of others in your school and community too. I would love nothing more than to become the team that fills lots of buckets on and off the court.

Jesus is our inspiration and motivation for being a bucket-filler. When He died on the cross, He emptied our buckets, which were filled with our sinful nature and sins, and replenished them with His love. Through His Word, the Holy Spirit fills our buckets with spiritual sustenance that is overflowing, a faith that gives us hope, peace, and joy.

Far too many people in this world allow their spiritual buckets to go dry or be emptied. Some try to fill their buckets with poison or garbage: drugs, alcohol, popularity, lies, sex, deceit, self-centeredness, false gods. Whether their buckets are empty or filled with harmful junk, they wonder why they feel disoriented or lost and cannot find any purpose, peace, or passion. Weakened and malnourished, their life and world breaks down and falls apart. If your bucket is empty, you have nothing to fuel your life.

You need to regularly hear and receive God's Word so that your spiritual bucket never goes empty but remains full and overflowing. By God's grace, stay in the Word. Read your Bible. Take the time for your personal devotions. Make faithful church attendance a priority in your life. Live and play with a bucket filled with God's love and grace, and then pour out the Good News to others. Remember, great players make lots of buckets while the Holy Spirit fills yours till it overflows. Bucket-filling is a beautiful thing.

A PRAYER FOR THE ATHLETES

Dear heavenly Father,

Thank You for Your grace and mercy and how You fill our spiritual bucket with Your love and forgiveness won by Christ for us on the cross. By the power of the Holy Spirit, may we be on the lookout for ways we can encourage one another and fill other people's buckets with Your Word and love.

In the name of the Father, the Son, and Holy Spirit, Amen.

Cutthroat

But I am afraid that as the serpent deceived Eve by his cunning, your thoughts will be led astray from a sincere and pure devotion to Christ. (2 Corinthians 11:3)

You are of your father the devil, and your will is to do your father's desires. He was a murderer from the beginning, and does not stand in the truth, because there is no truth in him. When he lies, he speaks out of his own character, for he is a liar and the father of lies. (John 8:44)

FOR THE COACH

Most basketball coaches have some sort of "cutthroat" drill, or game, that rewards players or teams for competing and battling with other players or teams. They call it cutthroat because the drill can get extremely intense and competitive in the pursuit of victory. Typical are cutthroat games that pit, for example, four teams of three players against each another. If your team makes a bucket, they take the ball and keep possession for another opportunity to score against the next threesome. Passion and energy flow. No one loafs. To get an easy score before the new team or defense can get set, the players inbound the ball quickly. Pressure to score and not allow the other team to score intensifies. Desperate players hack and foul opposing players in order to keep them from scoring while the coach swallows his whistle. Some players yell at their teammates as well as their opponents. Usually the losing players or team members receive some sort of punishment—sprints, sit-ups, or push-ups. An early water break and, perhaps, an extra shot of satisfaction might be the rewards for the team that wins in cutthroat.

The concept of cutthroat applies to our world beyond basketball too. Satan will do anything in his power to win and take us away from our heavenly Father. In our secular world today, many people try to downplay competition between worldviews or the spiritual war for our souls.

How's your scouting report on Satan? Many Christians overlook or disregard the toughest competition they will ever face on the schedule. Satan is determined to separate all of God's children from their heavenly Father permanently. A liar and a killer, Satan wants to devour and destroy you and the young people entrusted to your care. He plays for keeps, and we are in a cosmic battle for our souls whether we realize it or not. This is life cutthroat for all eternity.

You work hard to prepare your team for tough opponents—community rivalries, conference favorites, outstanding opponents, and so on—but are your student-athletes prepared for their fight against Satan? Is your program as committed to developing strong, rooted Christian leaders as it is an up-tempo offensive or defensive system?

The truth is your program blueprint, game plan, and talent will not be enough to defeat Satan. His offense is too potent. Moreover, you and your players' weaknesses—your selfishness, sinful flesh, failure to obey God, and so on—are glaring and will be unmercifully exploited by Satan.

Jesus, however, has already defeated sin, death, and the devil. Satan has his way with weaker opponents, but not Jesus. Jesus is undefeated and His record unblemished. When He went to the cross and died for your sins and the sins of the world, He crushed Satan one time for all time. In Christ is your victory!

Sometimes we forget that the game of life is spiritual cutthroat. We fail to see, in our comfortable and blessed life, that Satan is game-planning and will do anything to slit our spiritual throats.

As a Christian coach, your job is to prepare your young student-athletes for life beyond the court and the coming showdown, so share the Scriptures with your student-athletes. Make them memorize some favorite Bible verses and know them just as well as they are supposed to know your offensive sets and out-of-bounds plays. Have individual players pick different Bible verses that will be personal themes, emphases, or focuses for them throughout the season. (You can have them share and explain what their verses mean to them throughout the course of the year.) Encourage them in their church attendance and worship, Bible study, and prayer life. Put meaningful quality and quantity time into your team devotions. Confess your sins and apologize when you make mistakes. Show your players you are a sinner who relies on the Savior in your life too. Live with humility and gratitude. Remind them that while Satan plays life cutthroat, Jesus has already won eternal life for them on the cross. Point to the spiritual scoreboard and cross where the final score reads, "Jesus won, Satan zero."

A DEVOTION FROM THE COACH TO THE ATHLETES

Be sober-minded; be watchful. Your adversary the devil prowls around like a roaring lion, seeking someone to devour. (1 Peter 5:8)

Beware of false prophets, who come to you in sheep's clothing but inwardly are ravenous wolves. (Matthew 7:15)

You all know that I love to make you play cutthroat in practice. Cutthroat makes you play hard and brings out the real competitor in you. If you do not win, there is usually a punishment. To be successful, you have to hustle, be aware of what is going on, and communicate with your teammates. If your team is not ready to play when called upon, you will be out before you know it. The name of the drill itself is intentional, signifying that the drill is going to be a life and death ordeal.

Of course, you are not actually playing for your life in cutthroat, but what if you were? What if I said, "Winners move on, losers will be killed"? How would you play if you knew your actual life depended upon winning or losing the drill? Of course, you would play with the utmost intensity and urgency! You would cheat too, wouldn't you? You would grab, tackle, or do anything to stop the other team from scoring. Thankfully, the name of the drill does not represent reality.

There is a real-life cutthroat competition going on, however, between you and Satan. He truly wants to destroy and devour you and separate you from God permanently. This is why he tries to tempt you to skip church, forget your Bible reading and devotional time, and ignore your prayer life. Satan is playing and competing hard for your life! He is truly the most formidable opponent you or I will ever face, and someone whom we could never defeat on our own.

Praise God we do not have to vanquish the devil on our own. In this real-life cutthroat, this spiritual battle for our souls, we give thanks that Jesus has already defeated sin, death, *and* the devil through His death and resurrection. His victory is our salvation and our victory. No sprints, push-ups, or sit-ups required. Final score: Jesus won, Satan zero.

A PRAYER FOR THE ATHLETES

Dear heavenly Father,

Since Jesus' victory on the cross made us eternal winners, motivate us to serve others in Jesus' name. Send Your Holy Spirit upon us so that we may "work heartily" (Colossians 3:23) and give You glory in all that we do (1 Corinthians 10:31).

In the name of the Father, the Son, and the Holy Spirit. Amen.

Are They Still Touching the Line?

Take care, brothers, lest there be in any of you an evil, unbelieving heart, leading you to fall away from the living God. But exhort one another every day, as long as it is called "today," that none of you may be hardened by the deceitfulness of sin. For we have come to share in Christ, if indeed we hold our original confidence firm to the end. (Hebrews 3:12–14)

Keep a close watch on yourself and on the teaching. Persist in this, for by so doing you will save both yourself and your hearers. (1 Timothy 4:16)

FOR THE COACH

In order to get their players in peak playing condition, many coaches demand that their players run "ladders," "suicides," or organized sprints where players must touch the line with their foot or hand before they can reverse direction and finish the conditioning drill. "If you don't touch the line," you might holler during the first day or week of practice, "then we'll stop and run it again!" And you mean it. The season is young, and you want to establish discipline and good habits.

Coaches and players are usually very careful not to fall short of the line early in the season, but what about later in the season? Will you have the guts to discipline the entire team for a player who fails to touch the line in January as you did in November?

Great coaches get what they demand from their players, and nothing less. They pay attention to detail and demonstrate a total commitment to improvement, discipline, and mental toughness in their student-athletes. They also know that they are only as good as their word. Coaches who demand that players touch the line in wind sprints better make sure they stay true to their word. Players need to see that your word means something, that you, as their coach, not only talk the talk but walk the walk. Failure to discipline the team when a player does not touch the line reveals carelessness or, worse, a lack of resolve to do anything about it. Furthermore, if a coach is willing to look the other way or ignore players who cheat on wind sprints, what else is the coach willing to sell out on or neglect? When a coach fails to follow through on commitments, promises, or declarations, sloppiness seeps into all aspects of a program or team and might not be exposed until it is too late.

Christians face the same temptation in their daily faith walk too—they try to cheat God or take shortcuts in their spiritual lives. They start out on fire for their Lord or have that enthusiasm and childlike faith in God during their younger years in life, but then seem to slowly drift from the faith. They start missing church because of entertainment options, work, or other temptations and stimulation. The drift from church starts slowly and innocently enough—one Sunday missed here, another one there. After several months, however, they find themselves not even feeling guilty for skipping church. False doctrine, drugs, alcohol, sex, pornography, cradle-to-grave government dependency, and other temptations and philosophies replace the inspiration of God's Word. These once faithful churchgoers are not only failing to touch the line, but they also have quit the team!

Too many people give up or want a do-over when life ceases to be "fun" and entertaining. Teach your players determination, grit, integrity, trust, resilience, resoluteness, and so many other leadership and life skills by laying out your expectations and goals and working relentlessly to accomplish and fulfill them. They may not like running sprints all the way to the line or executing the little details of every drill, but they will never forget your dedication, focus, commitment, and faithfulness to the cause.

Even more important, watch over your players' faith lives with the same dedication and vigilance. Encourage your players to care for one another's spiritual lives even more than their athletic development. Do not let them cheat God, or themselves, by falling for Satan's insidious deceptions and distractions. Model the way and remind them to keep their eyes fixed on Jesus (Hebrews 12:2). Only by receiving God's grace, through His Word and Sacraments, can you and your players stay on the straight line or straight path of salvation. By God's grace, let Jesus touch you for all of eternity.

A DEVOTION FROM THE COACH TO THE ATHLETES

But I have this against you, that you have abandoned the love you had at first. Remember therefore from where you have fallen; repent, and do the works you did at first. If not, I will come to you and remove your lampstand from its place, unless you repent. (Revelation 2:4-5)

I have fought the good fight, I have finished the race, I have kept the faith. (2 Timothy 4:7)

One reason cheating is so tempting in our world today is that people can often get away with it—at least for a little while. When I ask you to sprint and touch the line or do certain little things in drills, you might get away with it if I'm not looking at you, right?! The reality is, however, that cheating on these drills, or failing to touch the lines, really only hurts you in the long run. Those drills and sprints are designed to help you play to the best of your ability. If you fail to touch the line or do the little things that can make a big difference in your play and performance, you are really cheating yourself.

The same is true for your faith. You can get away with cheating in your relationship with God for a little while. The pastor is probably not going to call your home if you miss church one Sunday. Your mother or father will not know or ground you if you fail to read your Bible or daily devotions this week. Slowly but surely, however, if you do not tend to your relationship with God, you will wake up one day wondering what happened to God and your faith life. As the old saying goes, if you feel distant from God, guess who moved!

Good athletes stay disciplined in their pursuit of improvement and touch the lines, just as Christian leaders stay in terrific spiritual shape when they remain in touch with God's Word and their relationship with Him.

Jesus could have changed His mind and backed off the line in the Garden of Gethsemane or on that first Good Friday. Yet He never wavered in His divine commitment to your salvation. There was no backing off the line—no fading, no let up, no shortcuts in Jesus' life and mission. He deliberately and intentionally shed His innocent blood to redeem you from your sins. Thanks to Jesus, we can finish the race, or sprint, here on earth and keep the faith.

A PRAYER FOR THE ATHLETES

Dear heavenly Father,

Send your Holy Spirit upon us in extra measure, Lord, so that our faith and relationship may not fade, but grow deeper in You. Help us look out for one another and encourage one another in our church attendance, Bible study, devotions, and prayer life so that we may continue to receive Your love and forgiveness in Your words of eternal life (John 6:68).

We ask this in the name of the Father, the Son, and the Holy Spirit. Amen.

SPRING

Proper Nutrition

Your words were found, and I ate them, and Your words became to me a joy and the delight of my heart, for I am called by Your name, O LORD, God of hosts. (Jeremiah 15:16)

Jesus said to them, "I am the bread of life; whoever comes to Me shall not hunger, and whoever believes in Me shall never thirst." (John 6:35)

FOR THE COACH

The emphasis on proper nutrition for athletes has come a long way. Not long ago, student-athletes at all levels would cap off a grueling practice by drinking a six-pack of orange or grape soda and consume a small pan of brownies because they were so thirsty and hungry. Football players consumed hot dogs and nachos during games, and baseball players chewed tobacco. Caffeinated drinks were often encouraged and served before a meet or match in order to stimulate an athlete's focus, alertness, and energy. Some coaches refused to let their players drink any water or liquids during practice in order to "toughen them up" or discipline them for sloppy play in practice.

Of course, we know better today. Whatever their age, student-athletes need healthy and wholesome nutrition. As the saying goes, if you put garbage in, you get garbage out. Performance will suffer and decline with a poor diet, as will one's overall quality of life. Furthermore, our society and culture are suffering from a crisis in health—obesity and eating disorders continue to rise in frequency and contribute to significant life challenges beyond a student-athlete's playing days. Therefore, great coaches teach their players the value of good nutrition and how to make it a part of their everyday life.

Just as a healthy diet is important to the productivity of an athlete, so also is a healthy diet of God's Word to the spiritual and emotional well-being of a Christian. The world is full of people who give words of advice—some good and some not so good—and teach false doctrine. Only Jesus, as revealed through Scripture, has "the words of eternal life." Only through the hearing and receiving of the Word of God does the Holy Spirit give us faith (Romans 10:17).

Junk food tastes delicious at the moment but leaves you hungry, malnourished, and craving wholesome sustenance when the sugar buzz or empty calories wear off. In the same manner, when we replace God's Word with sex, drugs, false teachings, and other spiritual and material idols, the momentary thrill of sin—a sugar high to be sure—eventually burns off and leads to a crash, suffering, and spiritual starvation. Our souls yearn for the substantive, healthy, close relationship that only Jesus and God's Word can provide. By the power of the Holy Spirit, we need to receive and consume the rich spiritual food that comes to us through God's Word and His body and blood. God was the first, preeminent nutrition expert.

One must eat properly on a daily basis. You do not just eat "right" one day and have your proper nutrition fill for the rest of the season. Put another way, do you remember what you ate for lunch last week Thursday? The point is that whatever you ate and drank in the past, it sustained and nourished you for that day. The same holds true for receiving God's Word. You might not remember the Scripture passages read in church three Sundays ago, but the Word of God, through the Holy Spirit, continues to work on your heart and mind and sustains you spiritually. God's Word nourishes you daily and is essential to your lifelong faith walk. Just as omitting food and drink for one day can be harmful to your physical body, skipping church and ignoring God's Word can lead to serious damage to your spiritual health and soul.

Encourage your players to eat and drink healthy foods for the good of their athletic productivity. Even more important, model and teach them to receive and consume God's Word each and every day. Only Jesus and God's Word will keep them in peak spiritual condition.

A DEVOTION FROM THE COACH TO THE ATHLETES

Or do you not know that your body is a temple of the Holy Spirit
within you, whom you have from God? You are not your own,
for you were bought with a price. So glorify God in your body.
(1 Corinthians 6:19–20)

So faith comes from hearing, and hearing through the word of Christ.
(Romans 10:17)

Hey, think about this for a second: What would happen if you did not eat or drink for a few days? Would you be able to perform at a top level or even make practice? We know the importance of eating and drinking healthy in order to sustain our mind, heart, and body. And this is especially true for you—athletes who make extra physical demands on your bodies. You will never become the best athletic performer you can be if you do not give your body the proper nutrition it needs to heal, grow, and remain energized. You have heard the old adage "If you put garbage in, you will get garbage out." All the strengthening and conditioning you do will be for naught, or seriously wasted, if you do not fill your body with healthy nutrition. The Bible says that your body is a "temple of the Holy Spirit" (1 Corinthians 6:19), so take care of it in a God-pleasing manner.

We know that we would never skip eating and drinking for a few days and expect to function well as an athlete. Yet too many people do not seem to be bothered about their spiritual heath in the same manner. If they skip church or Bible study, they do not think about the negative impact that has on their spiritual well-being and faith. They do not comprehend their own famished soul.

Just like our physical bodies, our souls need proper spiritual nourishment, which comes only through the Scriptures and Sacraments. Without God's life-saving and life-changing Word, we would not have faith. Or if we skimp on attending church or read our Bible only occasionally, our faith condition and relationship with God weakens and atrophies.

So let us encourage one another to feast daily on the rich and healthy Word of God in the worship service and in our personal Bible reading and devotions. By God's grace, let us stay in shape and peak spiritual condition and implore God to protect us against the power of the devil and our own sinful nature.

A PRAYER FOR THE ATHLETES

Dear heavenly Father,

Thank You for feeding us through Your Word, the words of eternal life. May we always recognize what Jesus, the bread of life, did for us on the cross and the forgiveness of sins that we received because of Him. Help us to encourage one another to feast on your Word and Sacraments in the worship service and in our own personal Bible study and devotional time so that our faith and relationship may be nurtured and strengthened in You.

In the name of the Father, the Son, and the Holy Spirit. Amen.

Making Contact

Your word is a lamp to my feet and a light to my path.
(Psalm 119:105)

So faith comes from hearing, and hearing through the word of Christ. (Romans 10:17)

It is the Spirit who gives life; the flesh is no help at all. The words that I have spoken to you are spirit and life. (John 6:63)

If you abide in My word, you are truly My disciples, and you will know the truth, and the truth will set you free. (John 8:31–32)

FOR THE COACH

Many coaches and fans agree that the most difficult skill to perform in sports is hitting a baseball. The batter must see the ball coming off the pitcher's delivery, recognize the pitch, determine whether to swing, and then actually make contact, or put the bat on the ball, all in under a second. Not to mention that the ball must be put in play in fair territory and hit away from the defense! Indeed, baseball players who *fail* to make good contact in seven out of ten at-bats are still considered all-star and Hall of Fame caliber players.

Making contact with the ball is a crucial and difficult skill. That is true in many other sports too. Golfers, of course, must strike the ball precisely to maximize distance and accuracy on their shots. A mark of a good volleyball team is a stellar serve receive and pushing up a good pass. Great basketball teams chart deflections accrued on defense and insist that their best offensive player "touches" the ball before someone else offers a shot attempt. Football players exercise sound "ball security" on offense and look to force turnovers on defense by touching or stripping the ball from ball carriers, quarterbacks, and receivers. Soccer coaches constantly exhort their players to "Go to!" the ball or touch the ball in order to control it and set up good passing lanes and approaches. And in the game of fastpitch or baseball, coaches reinforce the notion that making contact at the plate and putting the ball in play, especially with two strikes, remains fundamental for successful offensive play. As opposed to striking out, making contact moves runners over, forces the defense to make plays (or errors), and drives in runners on base. The bottom line is this: making contact with the ball is essential in many sports.

Even more important than making contact with the ball, making and staying in contact with your God is vital and indispensable to your faith. In fact, your faith will eventually strike out if you fail to make contact with Him. Hearing God's Word in the worship service, reading your Bible and devotionals, and lifting your prayers up to him regularly keep you in contact with your heavenly Father.

Unfortunately, too many people think they can be faithful or "good" without making contact with God. Can you imagine a baseball team winning a game without ever putting the ball in play? Would a golfer even get past hole number one without striking the ball? How could a volleyball team even score a point without receiving and returning a serve? How would a soccer team score or defend a goal without making contact with the ball?

As a coach, you drill and practice making contact with the ball regularly and repeatedly. You do not just practice hitting and putting the ball in play one time. Rather, your team practices hitting daily through various drills and repetition.

Our triune God loves His relationship with you—always guiding and guarding you. This is why He sent His Son, Jesus, to live among the people, make contact with His children in the flesh, and eventually die on the cross for you.

By the power of the Holy Spirit, may you be inspired to stay in direct contact with Him through His Word, Sacraments, and prayer. Indeed, keep your relationship with God in play eternally.

A DEVOTION FROM THE COACH TO THE ATHLETES

Man shall not live by bread alone, but by every word that comes from the mouth of God. (Matthew 4:4)

The grass withers, the flower fades, but the word of our God will stand forever. (Isaiah 40:8)

One of the reasons hitting a baseball is so exhilarating is that it is hard to do. In fact, many sports experts insist that hitting a baseball might be the hardest skill to execute in all of sports. You have to pick the pitch up out of the pitcher's hand and delivery, see the ball, determine if it is a strike or ball, and then swing and make contact, all in under a second!

Not only is it hard to make contact, but it is essential for good fastpitch or baseball teams to make contact and put the ball in play so that the defense is forced to make plays. They might make an error and put runners on base, or even if they get the batter, a ground ball or fly ball might score the baserunner from third.

Good teams make consistent contact with the ball, and not just in fastpitch or baseball. Soccer players must touch the ball and control it to establish passing lanes and offensive sets. Efficient volleyball teams possess an excellent serve receive and passing game. Football teams focus on ball security. Exemplary basketball teams strive for deflections on defense and make sure their best players touch the ball on every offensive possession. Of course, golfers must strike the ball and make solid contact every time for accuracy and distance. You get the idea: making good contact is essential in a lot of sports.

There is another kind of contact that is even more important, however, and that is staying in touch with God. Making and staying in contact with God is crucial to your faith and spiritual growth. By hearing His Word in church, reading the Bible or Christian devotions, and praying to Him, we remain in faithful contact with God.

Your parents ask you to stay in contact with them when you are out and about because they love you and want to make sure you are safe. Girlfriends and boyfriends stay in contact with each other because they like or love each other and want to bond. You use your phones and social media to stay in contact with your friends.

Make no mistake, God loves you and truly wants a close, personal relationship with you. So just as you work hard in practice and games to make contact with the ball, make regular and faithful contact with God, who sent His one and only Son to die for you and forgives you all of your sins. He wants you in heaven where you will stay in contact with Him forever.

A PRAYER FOR THE ATHLETES

Dear heavenly Father,

Send Your Holy Spirit upon us so that we may grow in our desire to make and stay in contact with You through Your Word, Sacraments, and prayer. Use us to lead others to make contact with You too.

In the name of the Father, the Son, and the Holy Spirit. Amen.

Statistics and Numbers

Are not two sparrows sold for a penny? And not one of them will fall to the ground apart from your Father. But even the hairs of your head are all numbered. Fear not, therefore; you are of more value than many sparrows. (Matthew 10:29–31)

But the LORD said to Samuel, "Do not look on his appearance or on the height of his stature, because I have rejected him. For the LORD sees not as man sees: man looks on the outward appearance, but the LORD looks on the heart." (1 Samuel 16:7)

FOR THE COACH

After a long, hard-fought extra-inning game, your players score an impressive victory, and you could not be more proud of your team's effort. Afterward, your players radiate joy and celebrate the crucial win, all except your starting third baseman. So why does he look so disappointed and dejected after such a huge win? You know exactly why: He took the doughnut and went 0 for 5, striking out at the plate three times. He could care less about the team win. His ego, as well as his stats and numbers, took a beating.

Individual statistics and numbers are an integral part of almost every sport. Baseball players "hit for average," count their RBIs (runs batted in), and tally their strikeouts from the mound. Cross-country and track runners strive for personal records (PRs) and focus on reducing their own times as well as beating their opponents. Shot and discus athletes measure the distance of their throws. Blogs and websites keep track of basketball and soccer scoring leaders as well as volleyball kills, assists, and digs. Football players receive stickers on their helmets for touchdowns scored, completions, and 100-yard rushing and receiving games.

Unfortunately, certain stats and numbers can overshadow critical tasks and efforts necessary for team success. The baseball player who sacrifices his own at bat to move the runner over to second; the lineman who never touches the ball but plows holes for his tailback to run through; the middle defender who never records a save, assist, or goal but relentlessly sacrifices her body to stymie opposing forwards in front of her goalie; the back-row specialist who never gets to serve or hit but keeps the ball in play—

these student-athletes and their actions do not make headlines or garner the interest or media coverage others receive, but they are crucial for team success and achievement.

One of the most important things you can do is repudiate and discipline an athlete who cares more about her stats and numbers, and the accompanying renown and glamour she craves, than being a team player. Obviously the more talented athletes on your team, more than likely, will accumulate impressive numbers and statistics as your season unfolds. At least you hope so! There is a difference, however, in the soccer player who takes the most shots on goal to help her team succeed and the player who wants a trophy, a headline, or to make a name for herself. Christ-followers put the needs of others ahead of themselves. Do not let the glamour groupie on your team give a false testimony of the selflessness and love of Christ.

Inspired by Jesus' love for each individual, recognize that each athlete brings something special to the team. Remind them that there are many different ways to "score" or accumulate stats and numbers for the team. Be creative and find ways to chart or record statistics that capture hustle and effort plays. Moreover, leadership, enthusiasm, encouragement, passion—these highly-valued attributes might not make the box score, sports' blogs, websites, or local newspaper, but they are treasured and noticed by teammates and fans alike. Encourage each athlete to pad his or her stats in these areas. Make sure you create a culture where teamwork, unselfishness, hard work, and servant leadership are recognized and highlighted by you and your players. As Scripture says, "Whatever you do, work heartily, as for the Lord and not for men, knowing that from the Lord you will receive the inheritance as your reward. You are serving the Lord Christ" (Colossians 3:23–25).

Finally, teach your student-athletes that the world often uplifts and touts superficial things that may *seem* important at the time but are really quite meaningless and trifling. Instead of the glitz and glamour of the outside world, God looks at your heart (1 Samuel 16:7). Remind your athletes that they are special, not because of how many points, goals, kills, aces, birdies, home runs, or first place finishes they statistically accumulate but because Jesus took all of their sins and zeroed them out when He died on the cross. Statistics and numbers do not matter to Jesus. You do.

A DEVOTION FROM THE COACH TO THE ATHLETES

So the last will be first, and the first last. (Matthew 20:16)

Let each of you look not only to his own interests, but also to the interests of others. (Philippians 2:4)

We live in a data-driven and YouTube world these days. There is an obsession with statistics and numbers and self-glorification—everyone wants to be first or accumulate the most shares or likes so that they can get their name mentioned in a tweet, blog, or newspaper. Glamour is good and desirable. Grunt work is boring and hard. To be sure, there is nothing wrong in striving for excellence and trying to finish first or get the most out of something.

Sometimes, though, our culture and society can lose track of what makes athletic teams successful and special. People often record and post video highlights of great scoring plays rather than defensive effort, sacrifice, or hustle plays. Have you noticed that individuals often ask how the game or meet went, and then quickly add, "So how many points did *you* score?" Or "how much time did *you* play?" "Did *you* start?" "How many goals, kills, yards, or hits did *you* get?" Our world loves statistics and numbers, especially the number one—me, myself, and I.

There are a lot of stats and numbers out there in our world today, but here are the ones that really count: God sent His *one* and only Son, Jesus, to die for *you* and *all* sinners. Your sins, too numerous to count, have been wiped clean and knocked down to zero thanks to the blood of Christ. Each of you is "fearfully and wonderfully made" in the image of God (Psalm 139:14), who loves you so much that He even knows the number of hairs on your head (Matthew 10:29–31). Run the analytics on all that!

God does not look at the glitz and glamour that the world looks at; He looks at the heart (1 Samuel 16:7). He made you special and in His image (Genesis 1:27). No one is exactly like you or ever will be. And God has blessed each of you with unique talents, skills, and gifts. We would not be the team we are without the specialness of each person in this room.

Jesus had the best statistics and numbers of anyone in history—no sins, no errors, no mistakes. Yet God sacrificed His Son for the good of the team, the good of humankind, which includes *you*. Inspired by the Holy Spirit, let us care less about numbers and statistics, glamour, and worldly affection, and more about our teammates, loved ones, the people around us, and our relationship with Jesus.

A PRAYER FOR THE ATHLETES

Dear heavenly Father,

Forgive us for our self-centeredness and the craving for worldly affection and praise. Send Your Holy Spirit to work on our hearts and minds that we might put You first, others second, and ourselves last.

In the name of the Father, the Son, and the Holy Spirit. Amen.

Playing Time

Therefore, my beloved brothers, be steadfast, immovable, always abounding in the work of the Lord, knowing that in the Lord your labor is not in vain. (1 Corinthians 15:58)

For while bodily training is of some value, godliness is of value in every way, as it holds promise for the present life and also for the life to come. (1 Timothy 4:8)

FOR THE COACH

No one needs to remind you that playing time is a central issue in almost every sport. Whether they would admit it or not, most parents care far more about their child's playing time than the overall team success. If they could choose, most parents would rather have their child be an all-conference player, bat leadoff, and play in the field the entire game than see the team win a state championship with their child occupying the bench or seeing infrequent pinch-hitting duty. The truth is that parents love one child on the team more than all the others combined, even though you, as coach, must love and care for them all.

Playing-time decisions depend considerably on experience, skill level, and the expectations you have for your team. Younger teams and leagues may demand or encourage a more equitable amount of playing time for student-athletes as participation is the focus. Most coaches ultimately have to decide on their philosophic approach to playing time: Is your program, or team, built to pursue winning or broader student-athlete contribution? While not always mutually exclusive (some basketball, soccer, or volleyball coaches might argue, for example, that playing more athletes improves team practices, morale, depth, and play over the long haul), you have to decide what your approach and focus will be for your own team.

A Christian coach can defend either approach to the playing-time question. On the one hand, a coach might sound caring and compassionate by insisting everyone will play almost equal time. God really does not care who wins a soccer match or baseball game, and there are many more important things in life than kicking a ball past a goalie or hitting a line drive in the gap. So let everyone play! On the other hand, a coach could remind his or her team that God has gifted each of them uniquely, and, therefore, the best and most talented athletes will play more, especially as the competition increases. The coach could insist that one of the best life lessons any young student-athlete can learn is that he or she might not always be able to do what he or she wants in life, but God has a special plan and a purpose for each of us.

On the playing time issue, take a long-view approach and leave a Christian legacy with your players:

◎ Be forthright and candid about their playing-time prospects. Christians are about truth. Therefore, be honest and treat your athletes with dignity and respect.

◎ In the spirit of Matthew 18, encourage your student-athletes to come to you if they think they should be playing more or if they disagree with your coaching decisions. Tell them how much you respect courage, conviction, and open conversation rather than distrust, silence, and a lack of communication.

◎ Acknowledge that making playing-time or athletic-participation decisions are difficult for you too. You love and care for all your athletes. They are all a part of the team and, more important, part of the Body of Christ. All have essential roles on the team.

◎ Give each student-athlete your most prized possession: your time. Invest in a lifelong relationship with each kid. Chances are good that some of your best role players or benchwarmers will make the best coaches and leaders in the future. They will remember how you led, taught, and handled difficult times and decisions, that you saw them as special individuals even if they could not score a goal, make a basket, set the ball, hit a home run, or run a relay for you.

◎ Finally, and most important, encourage your players in their Christian walk. Whether they play a lot or not, you can still share God's Word and pray with them each and every day. These kids can win and experience the joy of the Lord each day in practice, on road trips, and during team meals. God put these kids in your life, under your care, for a reason. Do not waste the opportunity.

Just as student-athletes get only a certain amount of opportunities to compete or play, you only get a certain amount of time and special moments with each of your players. Make them count.

A DEVOTION FROM THE COACH TO THE ATHLETES

For just as the body is one and has many members, and all the members of the body, though many, are one body, so it is with Christ. . . . On the contrary, the parts of the body that seem to be weaker are indispensable, and on those parts of the body that we think less honorable we bestow the greater honor, and our unpresentable parts are treated with greater modesty, which our more presentable parts do not require. But God has so composed the body, giving greater honor to the part that lacked it, that there may be no division in the body, but that the members may have the same care for one another. If one member suffers, all suffer together; if one member is honored all rejoice together. (1 Corinthians 12:12, 22–27)

It's really an honor and a privilege to coach you all. As much as I enjoy coaching, however, I have to admit that the playing-time issue or deciding who participates and competes in certain competitions is one of the hardest if not *the* hardest decision I have to make.

I know some of you wish you would or could play more, and I certainly do not wish to see any of you hurting or upset. Unfortunately, there are only so many spots, positions, or time available for everyone to play.

Since this is an important topic, there are three things I want to remind all of you in regard to playing time:

1. Come talk to me if you are having difficulties in accepting your role on the team. I admire courageous people, and I promise you that I will truly listen to you and consider what you have to say.

2. We would not be the same team without you. Whether you play or compete a lot or a little, you are special to me and this team.

3. Most important, remember that Jesus died and rose again for all of you. Your sins and mine are forgiven. Each one of you is a loved and special child of God, and that's how we

need to treat one another on this team too—as superstars and special children of God.

Let us remember that with God it has always been about who you are and not what you do. You are redeemed in Christ. Whether you play a lot or a little, I hope you always remember that you are cherished, loved, and bought with a price. You are valuable and special. And no amount of playing time changes that truth.

A PRAYER FOR THE ATHLETES

Dear heavenly Father,

We did nothing to deserve Your grace and mercy. We are not starters or nonstarters, first-stringers or second-stringers in Your eyes, but Your beloved children. Whether we play or compete a lot or a little, we know You love us, and we find great comfort and joy in this truth.

In the name of the Father, the Son, and the Holy Spirit. Amen.

Accountability

So then each of us will give an account of himself to God. (Romans 14:12)

Iron sharpens iron, and one man sharpens another. (Proverbs 27:17)

FOR THE COACH

It happens to every team as the season progresses—athletes look for the paths of least resistance, the easy way out, and different ways they can skip the challenging phases of practices. They start to cheat in drills and skip or ignore minute details when they think the coach is not looking. They fail to hustle in drills and when they move from drill to drill. They stop going to bed at an early hour to get their rest. They start eating the junk food they once eschewed. They stop taking the extra batting practice, shots on goal, or running extra repeats like they did during the early portion of the season. Rarely do they visit the weight room. Even your superstars exhibit a waning of intensity and discipline.

Great coaches hold their student-athletes accountable each and every day in practice because they care. A coach who ignores players' mistakes and bad habits and does not challenge them to grow and improve is a coach who does not care if players reach their own personal goals or experience success during games. Keeping expectations high and demanding excellence and commitment from players reveals a coach who truly has the athletes' best interests and the team's best interests at heart. You may have even said something to this effect: "If I'm getting on you in practice, it just means I care and want you to be the best competitor you can be." Most student-athletes understand and appreciate this sentiment.

Too many people in this world today refuse to be accountable for their words and deeds. They overpromise and under-deliver; they fail to meet expectations and follow through; they expect entitlements or handouts in exchange for little effort or subpar work. Moreover, too many "leaders" do not want to hold others accountable for fear of retribution, political correctness, economic discrimination, social ridicule, and persecution. Even more tragic, too many people today do not want to obey God or admit the truth of Scripture because they simply do not want to be accountable to His Word and Commandments. Why feel guilty or messy?

As a Christian coach, you can teach your student-athletes the importance of accountability and the difference it can make for the team and in their own personal lives. Teams and athletes who hold themselves accountable, or compete for coaches who hold them accountable to the highest standards, often succeed in grand and impressive ways. As a coach, you get what you demand, so demand accountability. You do not have to yell, scream, holler, and kick things to reinforce responsibility. Do not whine and complain when they do not do what you want them to do. If you believe in your philosophy and convictions deeply, then steadfastly lift up your expectations and enforce these expectations every day. You will never regret holding yourself and your athletes accountable.

Beyond your sport, you should also teach your players that God holds them accountable as His followers. Jesus says that "everyone to whom much was given, of him much will be required, and from him to whom they entrusted much, they will demand the more" (Luke 12:48). God has given you and your student-athletes many privileges, gifts, and talents, and He expects you to use these treasures and blessings with caring stewardship and devotion.

Therefore, hold your players accountable for their performance and team commitment. Challenge them to lead and serve as Christian leaders. After all, God has given each of them so much, including their salvation.

As you teach and preach accountability, however, remind them that God no longer keeps a record or account of their sins, thanks be to Jesus. They are forgiven (you too). This is important because no matter how hard we try to be accountable to God and follow His commands, we all are incapable of fulfilling the Law. Just like our play and coaching will always be flawed, so will our daily thoughts, words, and deeds. Thank God He sent Jesus to be accountable for our sins.

Rejoice with your athletes and celebrate Jesus. Hear His Word. Receive His grace. Hold yourself accountable to share this Good News using the coaching platform God provides you daily. You will never regret it.

A DEVOTION FROM THE COACH TO THE ATHLETES

And no creature is hidden from His sight, but all are naked and exposed to the eyes of Him to whom we must give account. (Hebrews 4:13)

Everyone to whom much was given, of him much will be required, and from him to whom they entrusted much, they will demand the more.
(Luke 12:48)

Great competitors and great athletes hold themselves accountable. They run their sprints hard, not just at the beginning of the season, but throughout each and every day. They do not cheat on repetitions or try to take shortcuts when the coach is not looking. They do not make excuses when they make mistakes or perform poorly but own up to them and execute a plan to improve. Athletes who hold themselves accountable keep the promises they made to themselves—with a lot of hard work and no regrets.

Unfortunately, too many athletes refuse to hold themselves accountable. They do not admit their mistakes but make excuses. Their poor performance or miscue resulted from someone else's shortcomings or mistakes. The referees or umpires messed up. The coach did not know what he or she was doing. The opponent was just too good. They were not in the mood to compete or play hard. The list of excuses is literally endless.

People in the real world disdain accountability too. Many want gifts and entitlements but do not want to pay or work for them. Others want to do whatever they want whenever they want with no restrictions and limitations. If something goes bad or wrong, that is not their problem. Someone else can clean up the mess. How convenient!

As you heard a minute ago from the Bible passage, Jesus expects much from those who have been given much—and that would be *you*. Thanks to His death and resurrection, your sins have been paid for and forgiven. God could have held you accountable for all of your sins, but He sent His Son to take your place. Jesus washed away your sins on Mount Calvary more than two thousand years ago. Set free by Jesus' blood and sacrifice, God calls on you and expects you to live with purpose. He wants you to truly use the gifts given to you so that others might know the Good News and Jesus' love for them. He expects much from you.

I expect a lot from you too. You have been given so much in this life, including an opportunity to compete in this sport and give a testimony to Christ's love. By God's grace, let's hold one another accountable to be the best teammates we can be and to live a life that glorifies our Savior.

A PRAYER FOR THE ATHLETES

Dear heavenly Father,

If You held us accountable for our sins, we would receive and deserve eternal damnation in hell. Instead, You intervened and sent Your Son, Jesus, to redeem us and cleanse us from all unrighteousness. Help us to encourage one another and keep one another accountable so that everyone stays focused and fixed on You, the Author and Perfecter of our faith. By Your grace, please make it so.

In the name of the Father, the Son, and the Holy Spirit. Amen.

The Agony of Practicing the Day after Defeat

Count it all joy, my brothers, when you meet trials of various kinds, for you know that the testing of your faith produces steadfastness. And let steadfastness have its full effect, that you may be perfect and complete, lacking in nothing. (James 1:2–4)

And after you have suffered a little while, the God of all grace, who has called you to His eternal glory in Christ, will Himself restore, confirm, strengthen, and establish you. (1 Peter 5:10)

But He said to me, "My grace is sufficient for you, for My power is made perfect in weakness." Therefore I will boast all the more gladly of my weaknesses, so that the power of Christ may rest upon me. (2 Corinthians 12:9)

FOR THE COACH

While losing a tough game or competition hurts, coming back and practicing the day after a heartbreaking loss or setback is often even more painful. Whether you lost by ten goals, in a shootout, in extra innings, during the last leg of a relay, or on the last hole, and whether the team played their best or played their worst and got "run-ruled," leading with energy and enthusiasm the next day at practice is one of the most difficult things you have to do as a coach.

Rare is it that an athlete feels or cares as much about winning and losing as the coach. Players experience a loss; coaches live with it. You know you cannot go back and redo or fix things, but yet you struggle to let go. You are exhausted, and you know your players are tired too. Your next meet or game is a few days away. Mentally and physically fatigued, the odds are strong that your players will not be excited or enthusiastic to practice tomorrow. And then you remember you have to actually prepare a practice plan. Truthfully, your emotions range from cancelling practice on the one end to calling for a two-a-day on the other.

As a Christian coach, you have a unique platform to model and teach what it means to be a Christian living in a fallen world. God never promised Christians that life would be easy and free of hardship. When things are going well, in life and with your team, it's easy to live as a cafeteria Christian, picking and choosing what works and tastes good to you. When we experience and endure suffering, pain, or real loss, however, that is when we realize just how frail and weak we truly are. We need a Savior who will love us. We need a heavenly Father who will provide for us and protect us. We need the Holy Spirit to strengthen our faith. We need our triune God.

Exemplary Christian coaches are at their best the day after a tough loss. Almost anybody can coach a practice after an outstanding win. Resilient Christian coaches, however, own and embrace the practices after tough losses or failures. Christians, after all, should be the kings and queens of comebacks. Your players will need to hold onto this lesson of faith throughout the rest of their lives when they truly experience life's hardships and setbacks—experiences much more severe and significant than loss in a game or meet.

After a tough loss, get back to work. Address your team's weaknesses. Push your student-athletes to improve and grow. Do not lower your expectations. Demand excellence. Most important, make sure you do not cheat your players and forget to teach them about God's grace and love. Take advantage of the moment to inspire the young people God has put in your care by reminding them that Easter Sunday comes after Good Friday. There is no stopping God's plan of salvation. His love for us is bigger than any hardship we might endure. Teach them how to come back from defeat and, by God's grace, win every day in life.

A DEVOTION FROM THE COACH TO THE ATHLETES

For this light momentary affliction is preparing for us an eternal weight of glory beyond all comparison, as we look not to the things that are seen but to the things that are unseen. For the things that are seen are transient, but the things that are unseen are eternal.
(2 Corinthians 4:17–18)

I know how to be brought low, and I know how to abound. In any and every circumstance, I have learned the secret of facing plenty and hunger, abundance and need. I can do all things through Him who strengthens me. (Philippians 4:12–13)

The Bible says that "the Lord is near to the brokenhearted and saves the crushed in spirit" (Psalm 34:18). Perhaps that is how you are feeling—crushed in spirit—after our tough loss. Hey, trust me, nobody likes to lose, especially the way we did. It hurts. Today is a new day, however, and we have two ways we can respond: we can either lament it or learn from it.

Let me remind you of something: no team was more discouraged after a loss than the disciples. After Jesus' crucifixion, they were distraught, overwhelmed, embarrassed, and scared. They hid in their community, fearing for their lives. The agony of defeat had left them without hope. Their friend, teacher, and leader—Jesus—was literally beaten, nailed to a cross, and sealed in a tomb. The worst part was that they had abandoned Him and fled. They did not believe His promise that He would die for them and wash away their sins (and yours too). Then Easter Sunday came, and the resurrected Jesus appeared and changed them forever. These very same disciples, who were so down and out after losing their Jesus on Good Friday, would set out to preach the Good News to the ends of the earth for the rest of their lives.

Jesus has a way of changing one's perspective on life. Inspired by our risen Savior, we can bounce back, we can push forward, and we can live for another day with joyful anticipation. We lost a game or competition, not our lives, not our place in heaven.

Real life is going to be full of tough losses that hurt more—trust me on this, folks. We live in a sinful, fallen world filled with sinful people. We will have hardship, suffering, and adversity in our lives. Some days we may not even want to get out of bed. Losses in our daily lives, however, no matter how brutal or painful, can eventually turn into real blessings if they compel us to rely more on Jesus.

So let us go to work today and use the gifts God has given us to the fullest. Let us make this setback the first step on a comeback. With a risen Jesus by our side, be assured that we can face whatever loss or challenge confronts us in our lives with peace, strength, hope, and confidence. This is "a day that the Lord has made, let us rejoice and be glad in it" (Psalm 118:24).

A PRAYER FOR THE ATHLETES

Dear heavenly Father,

Yesterday's loss hurt. Help us, however, to keep the proper perspective on what is most important in life: our relationship with You. When Your Son, Jesus, was crucified, it looked like a really bad loss. He suffered and died to pay for our sins. We give thanks for Your grace and mercy and for always being with us no matter what temporary losses or suffering we endure in this life. Thank You for being our Rock and Refuge.

In the name of the Father, the Son, and the Holy Spirit. Amen.

Saves

Because, if you confess with your mouth that Jesus is Lord and believe in your heart that God raised Him from the dead, you will be saved. (Romans 10:9)

For the word of the cross is folly to those who are perishing, but to us who are being saved it is the power of God. (1 Corinthians 1:18)

FOR THE COACH

Every soccer coach knows that great defense begins and ends with your goalie. A great goalie, after all, is the last line of defense—the last hope—to stop the opposing team from scoring. Outstanding goalies make incredible stops on breakaway attempts, they aggressively snatch the ball out of the air on corner kicks, and they direct the defense with clarity and confidence. Moreover, exceptional goalies make saves that very few others can make, and they do it at crucial moments in a match. The great ones, real difference makers, can make average teams good and great teams elite. They play at a different level to catapult their team to greatness.

Although the top-tier goalies certainly make their share of spectacular saves, successful and efficient ones make many more routine saves than breathtaking ones. To be sure, deflecting a shot on goal against a breakaway or on a shootout kick that would otherwise end the match, those rousing and dazzling saves, certainly draw immediate cheers and elation. Those marvelous saves would mean little, however, if the goalie botched an easy roller or flubbed a routine kick, one which most goalies could easily secure. In other words, exemplary goalies make both the routine and spectacular saves.

Coaches sometimes lose patience with player development when they do not see spectacular growth and instantaneous improvement. They cannot understand why their athletes do not learn the finer aspects of their sport more quickly and efficiently, especially after receiving such "exceptional" coaching instruction. On rare occasions, coaches do see rapid advancement or development, but in most cases, skill enhancement and athletic production and efficiency increase incrementally over time through proper repetition, muscle memory, brain development, experience, and growth in confidence. You become a great goalie daily, not in a day.

In the same way, our relationship with Christ is a daily blessing and necessity, not something we enjoy or need only for a day. As sinful human beings, we can confess our sins and receive and bask in God's forgiveness each and every day. Certainly, we benefit by hearing and receiving God's Word daily, not just for one day. These daily renewals, or "saves," may seem routine and mundane, but they remain essential for a Christian's spiritual sustenance and growth. Think about it this way: You may not remember what you ate on Tuesday or Thursday three weeks ago, but that food and drink maintained and nourished your body so that you could keep functioning and living. Sometimes people come to faith in mountaintop conversion experiences, perhaps receiving the Word on their deathbed, after a family tragedy, or some other unique moment. Most, however, hear and receive the Word regularly, daily, as the Holy Spirit works faith in their hearts.

Remind your young student-athletes that just like every save by your goalie—from the routine to the spectacular—is crucial to your team's success, so is the time you set aside daily to talk and listen to God. Reading your Bible or devotions for fifteen minutes each morning or night may seem humdrum and low key, but this is an important time to hear God's Word and receive His grace and mercy anew. Better than any top caliber goalie, God is really good at saves—you are one of them!

Coaches love goalies who make the routine saves because they are dependable. Even the best goalies, however, let one get by them occasionally. The greatest and most spectacular save in world history occurred on that first Good Friday when Jesus died on the cross to save the world—and you—from the consequences of sin. Jesus *did* save your life and scored a shutout on sin, death, and the power of the devil. Heaven and eternal salvation are yours, thanks to Jesus. Nothing, not even Satan or your sinful nature, can ever get past Him and His cross. Only Jesus can make that save.

A DEVOTION FROM THE COACH TO THE ATHLETES

For God so loved the world, that He gave His only Son, that whoever believes in Him should not perish but have eternal life. For God did not send His Son into the world to condemn the world, but in order that the world might be saved through Him. (John 3:16–17)

Whoever has the Son has life; whoever does not have the Son of God does not have life. (1 John 5:12)

We all know that a great defense gives a team a wonderful opportunity to win. Soccer teams that play terrific defense, must, of course, receive significant contributions from everyone on the field. With that said, we all know that goalie play is the most essential piece in the defensive puzzle. The goalie is the last line of defense, the last hope to stop the other team from scoring, and must deliver saves.

All of us like goalies who make all kinds of saves—the routine easy rollers that come their way as well as the spectacular, incredible ones. The reality is if our goalie makes two unbelievable saves, but allows two easy ones to go by, our team is no better off than if the goalie makes the two easy plays but not the two dazzling ones. In other words, every save—no matter how impressive or simple—matters.

The greatest save in human history occurred when Jesus Christ came into the world and died on the cross for you to redeem you. His death and resurrection were truly spectacular. Even the best defensive soccer teams or goalies let some balls get past them, but nothing got by Jesus on that first Good Friday. He notched a divine hat-trick: sin, death, and Satan were shutout. He cleansed you from *all* your sins. He did not let one remain. That is *the* save of all time.

While perhaps less spectacular or stunning than His death and resurrection, Jesus still provides for you and forgives you daily. He gives you His Word and the opportunity to receive His grace anew every week in church. He listens to your prayers. He knows what you are experiencing, feeling, and facing. He never leaves your side and protects you against the evil and cosmic forces of this world. Perhaps these daily save opportunities seem less magnificent and more routine than Good Friday or Easter Sunday, but they are just as special. His grace never stops overflowing. He never stops loving or rescuing you. Jesus is your Savior. That is what only He can do. He saves.

A PRAYER FOR THE ATHLETES

Dear heavenly Father,

Thank You for sending Your Son, Jesus, to save us from our sins and selfishness. Thank You for giving us Your Word, listening to our prayers, and protecting us each and every day. Inspire us to cherish the daily saves You continue to provide so generously to us. May we share Your love and Word with others so that the Holy Spirit can continue to save people from their sins and give them peace.

In the name of the Father, the Son, and the Holy Spirit. Amen.

Coaching with Conviction

Therefore do not throw away your confidence, which has a great reward. (Hebrews 10:35)

For I know that my Redeemer lives, and at the last He will stand upon the earth. (Job 19:25)

Trust in the LORD forever, for the LORD God is an everlasting rock. (Isaiah 26:4)

FOR THE COACH

One high school girls' basketball team got torched in their man-to-man defense in an early, season-ending playoff loss in March. Anticipating that their coach would look for something different to implement next season, such as a matchup zone defense, the players were both surprised *and* impressed when he retaught, retooled, and rededicated team summer practices to a relentless man-to-man pressure defense. Apparently, their coach really believed in this man-to-man stuff. One season later, this team's suffocating defense led them to playoff success and a culminating state tournament berth. Their coach's conviction and commitment to stay with what he deemed an important staple of success—a tough man-to-man defense—compelled and motivated them to improve and execute at a high level. Conviction is convincing.

Convictions are also compelling. Players can tell and sense when a coach believes deeply in something or is just going through the motions. When a coach *says* defense and pitching wins games but spends most of the practice time on hitting, players notice. When a coach *says* tardiness to a team meeting disqualifies one from starting but then starts the tardy quarterback anyway, players notice. In the same manner, if a coach *says* her Christian faith is important but never bothers to lead devotions or share personal testimonies of her faith with her team, players notice that too.

This is not to say that coaches should never adjust or change their defenses, offenses, or tweak their program policies and expectations. Go ahead and put in that new zone defense if you like. Dedicate more practice time to hitting. Change your tardiness policy if you like. The point is that God put you right where He did to lead and to coach—with strong beliefs *and conviction*. As one World War II naval commander put it: "When you are in command, *command!*"

As Christians, we know that the Holy Spirit continues to work on our hearts and minds for a rich, deep, maturing faith. Nowhere in the Bible does God ask for or praise wimpy Christians. God does not want Christians of convenience, those who feign devotedness on Sunday while bending to secular pressure during the week, but Christians of conviction. After all, the Bible says that any lukewarm Christian who "shrinks back" (Hebrews 10:38) at the first sign of adversity or ridicule will be spit out (Revelation 3:16).

That is why you hold such a place of prominence and importance in the lives of your student-athletes. In addition to the sport you coach, you teach and share the faith and God's Holy Word. You remind them how much they need Jesus as well as an active faith and church life. Thank God Jesus lived and acted with great conviction when He went to the cross to pay for our sins!

Your athletes will appreciate your coaching philosophy, knowledge, and passion for the game. They will respect you as their spiritual mentor for your Christian conviction and focus on Jesus. You actually stand for something meaningful. Furthermore, sharing God's Word and the love of Christ with young people has a way of soothing and inspiring the soul.

So lead and coach with conviction. Stay true to your coaching philosophy and, more important, persist—*with conviction*—in teaching the faith to your players. Your athletes will never forget it.

A DEVOTION FROM THE COACH TO THE ATHLETES

My righteous one shall live by faith, and if he shrinks back, My soul has no pleasure in him. (Hebrews 10:38)

For we know, brothers loved by God, that He has chosen you, because our gospel came to you not only in word, but also in power and in the Holy Spirit and with full conviction. (1 Thessalonians 1:4–5)

Legendary UCLA coach John Wooden often told the story of how he managed to stay in control of his players and teams during the turbulent 1960s, when individual self-expression reached an apex among many American collegians. His star player, Bill Walton, was one of those individuals who expressed his rebellious nature by growing long hair over the summer. When Coach Wooden, whose team rules included clean-cut, short hair, brought his star athlete into his office to remind him of this fact before the season began, Walton balked, claiming he had a right to self-expression. After Walton finished making his case, Wooden kindly told him that he respected his forthrightness and conviction . . . *and the team was going to miss him.* Message received. Walton came to the first day of practice with his hair trimmed to Wooden's specifications.

Both Bill Walton and John Wooden had convictions. We respect people who possess strong convictions, even people with whom we disagree. Most of us carry strong convictions on how we should do things around here—how we practice, how we compete, how we form and work on the fundamentals and habits crucial to our success, and how we should carry ourselves as student-athletes and Christian servant leaders.

As a Christian, you can live with great certainty and conviction because Jesus died for you and has forgiven your sins. Thanks to Jesus, you will be in heaven someday. That is His promise to you and me, and God has never broken a promise.

In our sport, if you are indecisive or not sure what to do, if you practice or compete without confidence or conviction, you are going to fail or not perform to the best of your ability.

Unfortunately, too many people today do not have convictions about anything—including their faith. They do what is convenient and easy. They stand for nothing and fall for anything. They only pick out their favorite desserts or junk food in the cafeteria line instead of the fruits and vegetables they need to be properly nourished.

Too many Christians also follow and obey God only when it is convenient or easy for them. The Bible tells us, however, that God does not want us to be convenient or "lukewarm" Christians, but followers who, by the power of the Holy Spirit, are clear about who Jesus is and what He has done for us, confident in God's Word and convinced of God's love and promises. If faith and Christian conviction come through hearing the Word of God, make sure you get to church and conduct your own personal Bible studies regularly. Let the Holy Spirit truly nurture your conviction, confidence, and certainty of Christ's love for you.

Remember, Jesus went to the cross with conviction. Betrayed, abandoned, ridiculed, beaten, scourged, spit upon, mocked, and crucified—He would not be denied. He willingly and intentionally died for you so that your sins would be forgiven and your salvation assured. That is leading and living with conviction. Conviction is compelling. Thanks to Jesus, heaven is assured. His love for you is that magnificent and profound.

A PRAYER FOR THE ATHLETES

Dear heavenly Father,

Conviction is a strong and compelling force, whether in sports or in any arena of life. We ask for the Holy Spirit to continually work on and strengthen our hearts and minds so we may stay close to You through Your Word, worship, and prayer and live with Christian confidence and conviction. Thanks be to Jesus.

In the name of the Father, the Son, and the Holy Spirit. Amen.

Fearless

The LORD is my light and my salvation; whom shall I fear? The LORD is the stronghold of my life; of whom shall I be afraid? (Psalm 27:1)

The LORD is on my side; I will not fear. What can man do to me? (Psalm 118:6)

FOR THE COACH

Fearless competitors inspire. The petite fast-pitch hurler who challenges hitters with her fastball, the undersized guard who takes punishment from the bigs while relentlessly driving the ball to the basket, the batter who "wears" the wild pitch to get on base, the kid who plays hurt for the sake of his team, the short outside hitter who uses her "springs" to ruthlessly pound the ball down the line, the forward who keeps taking critical shots on the net despite his goal-scoring slump, the cornerback who does not back down when guarding the top wide receiver in the area, the coach who plays her star player with four fouls and several minutes to go in a tight contest, the guard who takes the last shot with the game on the line, the hitter who wants to be up at the plate with the winning run on third and two outs—all of these are examples of fearlessness. Fearless athletes and coaches are special.

One reason we admire fearless athletic performers is because they represent a stark contrast to sinful human beings who often succumb to fears and anxieties in daily life. Indeed, we are afraid to admit our sins and mistakes. We stew about things we cannot control. We worry about what people may think of us. We fear failure. We worry about getting old or sick. We agonize over our job and income. We worry about relationships. We fear being lonely or unpopular. We fear trying something new or shooting for the moon because we might crash and burn or look bad in our attempt. Even as Christians, we agonize over what people might say or think about us if we share the Good News of salvation and the love of Jesus for all. We fear being labeled a Jesus freak, intolerant, conservative, homophobic, or on the wrong side of history for standing up for the truth of God's Word and the Christian faith. One reason the Bible says "fear not" hundreds of times is because God knows our sinful nature and human condition. (Incidentally, every time an angel appears in the Bible, the first two words are "fear not.") Anxiety and worry consume us.

As a coach, you prepare your athletes for competition or game situations so that they will not flinch, or be intimidated or surprised by anything the opponent does. You work on drills and skills that equip them for adversity. You build their confidence so that they compete without hesitation. You praise and encourage athletes for courageous play, relentlessness, and overcoming challenges. In other words, you help instill your student-athletes with a fearlessness that exudes confidence and inspires others.

You and your student-athletes face an even scarier and more formidable challenge beyond athletic competition: your own sinful nature and the power of the devil. Undeniably, you *should* be scared about sin, death, and the power of the devil because you cannot succeed or overcome these obstacles in life and for eternity on your own, and neither can your athletes. You *should* be fearful about your eternal salvation if it were only up to you.

The good news is that living with the peace that surpasses all human understanding and making it to heaven does not depend on us. When Jesus died on the cross and rose from the dead, He defeated sin, death, and the power of the devil for all time, for *you*. Thanks to Jesus, *you have nothing to fear.*

One famous saying in sports is that there is no "i" in "team." You should make that point with fear too. Tell your players that there is no "i" in "fear" either, because they are not alone. Fearless athletes are special. So are fearless, redeemed Christians. They have Jesus. Fear not!

A DEVOTION FROM THE COACH TO THE ATHLETES

Have I not commanded you? Be strong and courageous. Do not be frightened, and do not be dismayed, for the LORD your God is with you wherever you go. (Joshua 1:9)

Even though I walk through the valley of the shadow of death, I will fear no evil, for You are with me; Your rod and Your staff, they comfort me. (Psalm 23:4)

I love watching fearless athletes and players in all sports. There is something motivating and inspiring about seeing athletes rise after they fall, accepting the challenge of the big moments, and not being afraid to compete when overmatched by size or talent. The quarterback who has thrown three interceptions but keeps on firing the football—that's fearless. The softball or baseball player who steps up to the plate with the game on the line, winning run at third, and two outs—that's fearless. The undersized volleyball player who keeps attacking and hitting over bigger defenders—that's fearless. The point guard who takes a charge from a player who weighs one hundred pounds more than he does—that's fearless. The soccer player who injured her ankle last game but plays on it anyway because her team needs her—that's fearless. Fearless athletes truly inspire.

In all walks of life, we admire courageous and fearless people. Perhaps this is because we, if we are honest with ourselves, have fears about many things in life. Maybe we are afraid to be alone, unpopular, criticized, ridiculed, looked down upon, or simply ignored. Death, rejection, pain, hurt—none of us want to think about or endure any of these things. Fear can shut us down or cause us to say things or do things we later regret, so when we see student-athletes, or anyone, exhibit and demonstrate courage and fearlessness, they impress us.

Out of all the fears in life, however, the worst fear any of us could have is living and dying without knowing Jesus Christ as our Lord and Savior. That would be truly scary. Life is hard in our fallen world—full of sin, selfishness, evil, and cruelty—and, thus, we want and need a loving, caring, sensitive Jesus by our side. Furthermore, none of us want to spend eternity in hell, a place where there is only torment, pain, aloneness, and, most critically, no Jesus.

In the history of the world, there has never been anyone more fearless than Jesus. In addition to ridicule, persecution, and a gruesome crucifixion, He carried and endured all of the sins of the world. Having defeated sin, death, and the power of the devil, Jesus secured your salvation for all eternity. Therefore, you can live a fearless life here on earth until you are called home to heaven. Just as there is no "i" in "team," there is also no "i" in "fear." Put another way, you have absolutely nothing to fear because Jesus was fearless for you.

A PRAYER FOR THE ATHLETES

Dear heavenly Father,

Help us to turn to You for comfort and peace when our fears and anxieties get the best of us. Encourage us to live a fearless life, knowing that Jesus took care of the most important thing (MIT), our salvation, when He died and rose again. Empower us to lead and serve as courageous Christians who share our fearless and brilliant Savior in an otherwise scary and dark world.

In the name of the Father, the Son, and the Holy Spirit. Amen.

Blessed and Inconvenient Interruptions: Spring Breaks, Proms, and Class Trips

I say this for your own benefit, not to lay any restraint upon you, but to promote good order and to secure your undivided devotion to the Lord. (1 Corinthians 7:35)

The fear of the LORD is the beginning of wisdom; all those who practice it have a good understanding. His praise endures forever! (Psalm 111:10)

FOR THE COACH

The new soccer coach called a meeting for girls interested in participating in spring soccer. With the coach nervous and wanting to make a good first impression, the gathering started better than expected. He connected with the girls and even sensed enthusiasm for the changes and new program vision. When he finally handed out the March practice schedule, however, his bubble burst. Several girls told him that they would not be able to practice for a week. They would be in Florida, Arizona, the beach—anywhere but here for spring break. "We have a game that first Tuesday after spring break," the coach insisted. The girls smiled, but ocean waves, sunbathing, and fun time with family and friends awaited. They seemed much more excited about flying south rather than flying around on the soccer field. No wonder the program had struggled the coach thought. These girls did not seem to be serious, committed athletes.

Although coaches compete against calendar conflicts in every season, spring is particularly challenging. The dynamic of coming out of the long winter months, the proliferation of different sporting options as the weather warms, the innumerable end-of-school-year award ceremonies, class trips, and various other activities, along with the reality that many families love to travel and vacation over spring break present plenty of calendar competition and conflicts for coaches.

Of course, the skill level and age of athletes you coach certainly do impact how you approach and handle these calendar conflicts. Expectations and commitment for a fifth-and-sixth-grade baseball team differs greatly from the expectations and commitment level one seeks from a varsity soccer team. And you should reward student-athletes in some way who do not have the privilege to travel for spring break but who show up every day for your grueling first few weeks of practice in the new season. There is no doubt that athletes who miss practice indeed fall behind in their preparation and skill development. Moreover, you do expect your student-athletes to be dedicated to their craft and team. Playing and competing on a team is a privilege and a sacrifice. Not everyone wants to be a successful student-athlete. Sacrifice and hard work are required!

Conversely, coaches who place too much importance on their own coaching ability and their own terrific practice planning often inadvertently teach their young student-athletes the wrong life lessons. Christian coaches, especially at the beginning of the year in their parent-coach meetings, often explicitly or implicitly tell families and athletes that their priorities are God, family, school work, and then their sport. When a family vacation to Florida interrupts and competes with their practice schedule, however, they conveniently forget to walk their talk. Instead, they make their student-athletes feel guilty or question their commitment to the team. The message is received loud and clear: sports, or coach's priorities, are more important than family vacations or once-in-a-lifetime class trips.

Perhaps God provides these inconvenient interruptions for you and your team's spiritual well-being and benefit. After all, today's world is obsessed with sports. Super Bowl Sunday is almost a national holiday and the most widely viewed global event of the year. Sports dominate radio talk shows, television, blogs, social media, and newspapers. Coaches cannot understand why their athletes do not care about winning or success as much as they themselves do. Student-athletes, or jocks, receive many intended and unintended social privileges and advantages compared to their non-athletic peers. Parents obsess over camps, coaching decisions, playing time, and their own self-esteem based on their kid's sports' acumen and success. Maybe inconvenient interruptions are blessed reminders of the priorities and values we need to teach and model to our young people. If only we would fixate and reflect as much on our relationship with Jesus Christ and our church involvement as we do about who's doing what camp and when this summer.

Be careful that you do not obsess over idols, including sports, more than your faith and family. On the other side of the coin, make sure your relationship with God is not just a spring break, prom, or class trip kind of relationship—infrequent, once-a-year, when we feel like it. God wants your heart and mind every day of the year. He wants you in church to receive His grace and mercy each week. He wants to hear from you in prayer and to talk to you through His Word. Sometimes it takes blessed and inconvenient interruptions to jar us back to our priorities and what really matters in life. Sports remain a wonderful gift from God, but they are not to become our god. Rest instead in God's grace for you. He has given you the Word of life. He loves you more than you can imagine.

A DEVOTION FROM THE COACH TO THE ATHLETES

Be still, and know that I am God. I will be exalted among the nations, I will be exalted in the earth! (Psalm 46:10)

But I have this against you, that you have abandoned the love you had at first. Remember therefore from where you have fallen; repent, and do the works you did at first. If not, I will come to you and remove your lampstand from its place, unless you repent. (Revelation 2:4–5)

During the season, I know we will face many distractions and interruptions. You all have a lot more going on in your life than just this team or sport. I get that. And actually, it is a real blessing from God that you are involved in so many other aspects of church, family, and school life than just this sport.

Make no mistake, however, I expect a lot of each of you. If you want to be good at anything in life, you have to practice and work at it, so I will be that coach who is relentless about individual and team growth and improvement.

With that said, I also believe sports can become too important in one's life, including my own. We do not want to make our sport our god. Faith, family, school work, and then this team, in that order—these are the priorities of our program.

While I do not like to see anyone miss practice, I want you to enjoy vacations with your family. Have a great time and be safe at prom. Cherish and have fun on your class trips. When you return, be ready to get back to work and make the most of the time God gives us together as a team. Most important, whether you are on vacation, at prom, on a class trip, or at practice, never forget the most important thing in your life is your relationship with Jesus.

No matter where we go or what we do, let us never abandon or forget Him.

A PRAYER FOR THE ATHLETES

Dear heavenly Father,

Thank You for interrupting our lives with reminders about what is most important in life—and that is our relationship with You. Thank You for sending Your Son to rescue us from our sins. His coming was a life interruption and intervention that we needed for eternal salvation. Someday, thanks to Jesus, we will make our road trip to heaven and be with You for all of eternity. We praise You from whom all blessings flow.

In the name of the Father, the Son, and the Holy Spirit. Amen.

Fairness

My brothers, show no partiality as you hold the faith in our Lord Jesus Christ, the Lord of glory. For if a man wearing a gold ring and fine clothing comes into your assembly, and a poor man in shabby clothing also comes in, and if you pay attention to the one who wears the fine clothing and say, "You sit here in a good place," while you say to the poor man, "You stand over there," or, "Sit down at my feet," have you not then made distinctions among yourselves and become judges with evil thoughts? Listen, my beloved brothers, has not God chosen those who are poor in the world to be rich in faith and heirs of the kingdom, which He has promised to those who love Him? (James 2:1–5)

He has told you, O man, what is good; and what does the LORD *require of you but to do justice, and to love kindness, and to walk humbly with your God? (Micah 6:8)*

FOR THE COACH

"How come my kid comes in the game, makes one error or has one bad at bat, and then you pull him out? Your starters can make all kinds of mistakes and still stay in the game! How is that fair?"

Sound familiar? If you have coached long enough in any sport, you certainly have heard this charge or complaint.

The truth is, in most cases, the parent who complains about this situation probably has a point. You do give star athletes a longer leash, or more opportunities, to work through their mistakes compared to role players with less talent; and this reality can, admittedly, give the impression that you are being unfair. Parents blame you for their child's discontent. You are a confidence killer.

There is solid rationale, however, for your playing-time decisions. Your starters play more because they possess more advanced skills than others, can execute more efficiently, and have greater potential to excel at a high level of play. You have observed them over hours of practice time, which parents do not see or consider. Put another way, these student-athletes, in your judgment, have greater upside or potential to impact the competition than the ones who are less skilled and talented.

Of course, you should self-assess and ask yourself if you treat your athletes fairly. We all have favorites and blind spots. In any event, unless you are coaching lower or middle grade school levels, which lend themselves to a more equitable playing-time understanding, you need to be prepared to address this charge honestly and from a Christian worldview perspective. Nowhere in Scripture does God say everyone deserves an equal opportunity or equal outcome here on earth. Is it really God's plan and desire for everyone to play equal minutes in a soccer match? Perhaps one of the most important things you can do is to help your student-athletes discover their gifts, strengths, and purpose beyond sports.

Teaching young people the concept of delayed gratification is also a worthy endeavor. They need to learn that they will not always get what they want when they want it in life. The same goes for an athletic team. Not everyone can start. Not everyone can play the most minutes. Not everyone can be an all-conference player. All athletes, however, can use and apply their God-given gifts and talents for the good of the team. In this way, they learn the value of God-pleasing stewardship, vocation, humility, and servant leadership.

As Christians, we thank God for His unfairness toward us since we deserve eternal damnation, death, and a permanent residence in hell. Yet, because He loved us so, God sent Jesus to redeem us. Jesus did nothing to deserve the scorn, ridicule, scourging, spitting, and crucifixion He endured. He definitely got the short end of the stick, or tree, on Mount Calvary. His loss, however, was our gain. Remind your student-athletes about how unfair life was for Jesus on Good Friday, and how we give thanks that God did not treat us fairly. Our heavenly Father played no favorites—He sent Jesus for all of us. Thus, we all can celebrate and rejoice in God's *unfair* plan of salvation!

Another aspect for you to reflect upon: are *you* being unfair to your players, or cheating them, by not sharing the love of Christ and God's Word, given the unique platform God has provided you? The good news is that you can do something about sharing the Good News!

Do your best to address the "fairness" issues directly, candidly, and kindly with your players and their parents. More important, do not miss the opportunity to talk about how Jesus treated us very unfairly, and we are blessed and grateful He did. Thank God that life is not fair!

A DEVOTION FROM THE COACH TO THE ATHLETES

As each has received a gift, use it to serve one another, as good stewards of God's varied grace. (1 Peter 4:10)

So the last will be first, and the first last. (Matthew 20:16)

Often times in life, we feel unfairly treated. Maybe we have even said, "Life just isn't fair." And sometimes, we really do get the short end of the stick. People might lie or take advantage of us or just plain not give us a fair opportunity. It hurts when we feel we are being treated unfairly.

As hard as we might try, as much as I try to be fair as your coach, we live in a fallen, sinful world that is often not fair. We see "good people" often get taken advantage of, lied to, or abused. I'm sure you've heard the saying, why is it that bad things so often seem to happen to "good people," and often times it seems that good things happen to "bad people"?

As Christians, however, we need to look at fairness from a biblical perspective. Since all of us are sinners, we deserve death and eternal life in hell. That is what is fair. None of us keep God's Commandments. No one can live a perfect life like Jesus did. God says that the wages of sin is death (Romans 6:23), and since He is our Judge, that is what we deserve. If we cannot follow His rules, we deserve His wrath and punishment.

Thankfully, though, God *did not* treat us fairly. We *did not* get what we really deserved. He sent His Son, Jesus, to take our punishment. Talk about bad things happening to good people! He paid the price on the cross for our sins. That was not fair to Jesus. He never sinned. He did nothing wrong. Yes, that is how much God loves you.

A PRAYER FOR THE ATHLETES

Dear heavenly Father,

We give thanks that You did not treat us fairly. We deserve Your wrath, punishment, and eternal damnation. Instead, however, You showed us grace and mercy through Your Son, Jesus, who died on the cross to forgive us all our sins. May we always be reminded, even when we feel someone treats us wrongly or unfairly, that You have eliminated all our wrongs and sins thanks to Jesus.

In the name of the Father, the Son, and the Holy Spirit. Amen.

Sportsmanship

*In the way of your testimonies I
delight as much as in all riches.
(Psalm 119:14)*

*How beautiful are the feet of those who preach the good news!
(Romans 10:14–15)*

FOR THE COACH

If a stranger or community member walked into your gym or on your field to watch your team compete, would this individual be able to tell which team and fan base represented a Christian school or organization?

When the all-time Yankee great Joe DiMaggio was asked why he always played so hard, he responded that there just might be fans at the game who had never seen him play before. He did not want to disappoint them or let them leave the park without knowing that he ran out every ground ball and played as hard as he could.

You should feel the same sentiment in regard to your team's sportsmanship and Christian testimony in the community. As the leader of your team, help your athletes understand that they are being observed in everything they do: the way they warm up, how they interact with umpires or officials (especially after bad calls), how they react to a tough loss or lopsided win, what they do when opponents take cheap shots at them, and when they are heckled by indecent fans.

One of the ways you and your team can use the platform God has given you is to exhibit and demonstrate Christian sportsmanship. People take notice of hustling, hardworking, respectful, humble, and focused student-athletes, no matter the score or outcome of the competition. Magnanimous, gracious, and grateful athletes, as they interact with fans and media after the game, also shine brightly in a self-absorbed world. Encouraging and uplifting coaches stand out compared to whiny, cussing, or hollering coaches who act as if they are supreme gifts to the profession. Moreover, great sportsmanship moments often present themselves during hard-fought games or meets that end in agonizing defeat. When your athletes thank and shake the umpires' or referees' hands after a poorly officiated match or game, when they compliment the opponent for stellar play instead of complaining about their own mistakes, when they hustle no matter how lopsided the contest, when they pick up an opposing player who just got knocked to the ground—these behaviors and actions make a profound witness and statement.

Mistakes will occur in sports. Emotions will provoke the old Adam and inhibit good judgment and decisions. Do not be afraid, however, to make the most of these sinful moments to demonstrate Christian leadership. One of the most powerful sportsmanship examples you can model is to apologize and make amends when you say or do something inappropriate to your student-athletes, parents, fans, opponents, umpires, or referees. Confessing your sin or mistake and then remembering and receiving God's forgiveness and absolution anew—these are pillars of Christian living.

You and your team can shine and reflect God's radiant forgiveness in a very dark world. Your team might not be able to win every game or place well in every competition, but you can always give a Christian testimony with class, humility, and exemplary sportsmanship. Others will notice, and God will bless your efforts.

A DEVOTION FROM THE COACH TO THE ATHLETES

Only let your manner of life be worthy of the gospel of Christ, so that whether I come and see you or am absent, I may hear of you that you are standing firm in one spirit, with one mind striving side by side for the faith of the gospel, and not frightened in anything by your opponents. (Philippians 1:27–28)

I appeal to you therefore, brothers, by the mercies of God, to present your bodies as a living sacrifice, holy and acceptable to God, which is your spiritual worship. (Romans 12:1)

The game raged back and forth between two equally matched college basketball teams. The contest was quickly morphing into a classic, a donnybrook, one for the ages. Tied after regulation, the game went into overtime. Then double overtime. The players were exhausted, but both teams were determined not to lose. With only a few seconds remaining in the double overtime, the home team was down two, but they had possession. They could tie the game with a two or win it with a three. An errant pass, however, forced a collision and the ball skipped out of bounds with eight seconds remaining in double overtime. Both officials looked at each other. They were not sure what to call. Then one referee did something unusual. He went up to a home-team player who was involved in the collision and asked: "Did the ball go off of you?"

The home-team player looked the referee straight in the eyes and replied, "Yes it did, sir." A possession and two free throws made later, the visiting team escaped with a four-point win in double overtime. To this day, most of the players who played for that team do not remember their record or the final score that day. They do recall, however, the courage and witness of a Christian teammate who could not tell a lie even if it meant losing a game.

When you play or compete in athletics, there is only so much you can control, including winning. One thing that you can do each day or night is demonstrate good sportsmanship and show people that there are more important things in life than winning or losing a sports competition.

In fact, what we say or do after a tough loss reveals more about our character and faith than when everything goes right and we win. It's easy to be magnanimous, nice, and generous when you win. But how about after a contest where the umpire or official makes a bad call that costs you the game? Or when you did not play your best? Or when the opposing team acts like jerks or the opposing fans taunt and ridicule you mercilessly? Or when you lose a race, competition, or game that you put your all into and really wanted? Then, how do you talk and act?

Jesus exhibited the most incredible sportsmanship and character ever on His way to the cross of Calvary. He did nothing wrong, yet was sentenced to death. Taunted, spit upon, ridiculed, scourged, abandoned by His teammates or disciples, and eventually crucified, He did not lose His temper or talk smack. He did not fight back. He did not yell at or backstab His heavenly Father or disciples. He simply responded with pure class and love in the face of total unfairness and a horrific execution: "Father, forgive them, for they know not what they do" (Luke 23:34).

Inspired by Jesus' sacrifice and words, may we all exhibit sportsmanship in our athletic competitions. May we demonstrate a Christlike humility and love for people, forgiveness, and the realization that the most important victory in life is already ours thanks to Jesus.

A PRAYER FOR THE ATHLETES

Dear heavenly Father,

Often our words, actions, and behavior do not represent or give a good testimony of You. We confess and repent of these sins and ask for Your forgiveness. Help us to realize and embrace the opportunity You give us to demonstrate Christian sportsmanship. Give us the courage, the stamina, and the desire to be salt and light in our competition and in our interactions with the community. Give us the wisdom and strength to model and demonstrate Christlike attitudes and love and, if the opportunity presents itself, to share the Good News with others.

In the name of the Father, the Son, and the Holy Spirit. Amen.

Handing Off the Baton

You shall love the LORD your God with all your heart and with all your soul and with all your might. And these words that I command you today shall be on your heart. You shall teach them diligently to your children, and shall talk of them when you sit in your house, and when you walk by the way, and when you lie down, and when you rise. (Deuteronomy 6:5–7)

Tell to the coming generation the glorious deeds of the LORD, and His might, and the wonders that He has done. (Psalm 78:4)

FOR THE COACH

The relay race is one of the most thrilling events in all of sports. While we understandably focus on the enthralling photo-finish endings of these races, track coaches know that most relays are won or lost in the seemingly routine baton exchanges between runners. Whether they use an up-sweep, down-sweep, push pass, or some other technique, runners who struggle or get bogged down with the baton exchange lose critical seconds. Worse yet, if the exchange occurs outside of the changeover box, your team is automatically disqualified. Even if you are not disqualified, a fumbled or dropped baton usually guarantees a last-place finish. Thus, track coaches spend a great deal of time teaching the baton exchange and having their athletes consistently practice this crucial part of the race. After all, if your relay team does not finish the race with the baton, you will not receive the prize or step up on the winner's stand or stage.

In the relay race of life, Jesus is the only one who can get you over the finish line. His sacrifice on the cross, the shedding of His precious and innocent blood, redeems you and awards you the ultimate prize and winner's circle—a blessed eternal life with Him in heaven. The odds are that if you are reading this devotional thought, you already know this truth.

Caring, dedicated Christian coaches, however, go one step further and make it a priority to hand off the baton to their student-athletes. They share God's Word and the love of Christ as regularly and routinely as they teach the fundamentals of their sport. They lead the team in Bible study or devotional readings and encourage their team leaders and captains to do the same. They pray together and encourage one another in worship attendance. The handing off of this spiritual baton is bigger than any relay race and way more important than any athletic accomplishment.

Just as track coaches demonstrate and model proper baton handoffs and exchange techniques before they make their athletes practice and hone these skills, God calls you to do the same in regard to your own faith life. Your student-athletes cannot receive the baton if you drop it or even refuse to run the race. The only thing worse than a DNF (did not finish) in a relay race is a DNS (did not start). Are you ready to take your mark? God put *you* right where He did to help your student-athletes improve in the sport to be sure. More important, He gives you a golden opportunity to share Jesus and God's Word as you encourage your student-athletes in their own faith walk.

As a Christian coach, God is calling on you to go first, to run the first leg of the relay, to initiate the devotions, Bible studies, prayer time, and faith talks with your athletes. They look up to you and respect you (and maybe even like you). Your actions and leadership speak volumes to impressionable, young student-athletes. Do not drop the spiritual baton or fail to hand it off.

The very act of handing off the baton from one runner to another is often called the exchange or "changeover." There is nothing that will change your life or the lives of your athletes more than God's Word and Jesus. On the cross, the Great Exchange took place. Jesus exchanged His life for yours.

So start out strong in your coaching race. You have received the baton from God. Run strong with it. Confidently hand it off to your athletes. Let them run with God's Word as the Holy Spirit fills them and nurtures their faith. Watch them grow closer to Jesus as your season enters the final lap. Let them run the "anchor leg," or last leg, of the race anchored in their Savior. On the victory stand, thank God for His unending grace and mercy. At your closing team banquet or bust-up party, celebrate and cherish the fantastic finish awaiting all who run for the prize (Philippians 3:14) and the everlasting life to come.

A DEVOTION FROM THE COACH TO THE ATHLETES

I charge you in the presence of God and of Christ Jesus, who is to judge the living and the dead, and by His appearing and His kingdom: preach the word; be ready in season and out of season; reprove, rebuke, and exhort, with complete patience and teaching. (2 Timothy 4:1–2)

But lay up for yourselves treasures in heaven, where neither moth nor rust destroys and where thieves do not break in and steal. For where your treasure is, there your heart will be also. (Matthew 6:20–21)

The best relay teams do an excellent job of handing off the baton. This exchange does not happen automatically. They practice it regularly because they know that the baton must be shared in order to achieve the best time and to win the race as a team. If you drop the baton or do not pass it properly, your relay team can be disqualified. The bottom line is that you cannot win a relay race without handing off or sharing the baton.

By God's grace, each of you have received something that is even more special and precious than the baton used in a relay race—and that is Jesus. Jesus rescued you from your sins and the sting of death. He crossed the finish line for you in the race for eternal life. The ultimate victory is yours, thanks to Jesus. When your time here on earth is done, you will be called to your heavenly home to be with Jesus in all of His glory. What a victory celebration that will be.

Until that final victory lap, however, God has wonderful plans for you, and He expects much of you too. He's given you His Word, His promise, His assurance that you are redeemed and set apart. Furthermore, God wants you to share the baton and hand it off to others. He wants all runners and people in this world to receive His love and grace and run with these. With Jesus, everyone wins.

Don't hide or drop that baton. Don't wait to hand it off until it is too late. That runner, that person, may never receive it if you don't pass it on. Run your race. Share God's love and Word. The more you do it, the better you will get at it. God will bless your efforts. He loves good relays and great exchanges, especially ones that really matter for all eternity.

A PRAYER FOR THE ATHLETES

Dear heavenly Father,

Thank You for sending Jesus into the world to pay for our sins. Give us the awareness and courage to hand off the baton, to share Jesus' love and Your Word with others. May they know the joy, peace, and victory we have thanks to Jesus.

In the name of the Father, the Son, and the Holy Spirit. Amen.

Overtime, Shootouts, Extra Innings, and Sudden Death

I shall not die, but I shall live, and recount the deeds of the LORD. *(Psalm 118:17)*

When Jesus had received the sour wine, He said, "It is finished," and He bowed His head and gave up His spirit. *(John 19:30)*

FOR THE COACH

One blessing of overtimes, shootouts, or extra-inning games is that you and your team get to play more of the sport you love. For coaches and athletes who love to compete, especially with the stakes elevated, more is better.

Another aspect of overtimes, shootouts, and extra-inning games are that they remind us of the preciousness and fleeting nature of life. Games and matches can end dramatically and suddenly. A pick-six, a header off a corner kick, a homerun, or an error can end the game in a gut-wrenching fashion. Momentum can suddenly shift with a great hustle play for a free ball, turnover, or hand ball in the penalty zone. The point is that any time a team enters an overtime period, shootout, or extra-inning game, the stage is set for a sudden ending and finality.

As you coach your student-athletes over weeks, months, and possibly even years, pay attention to their life momentum. Compliment and nurture your athletes when you see positive growth, good decisions, leadership development, and overall maturation. If you see their life path changing for the worse due to bad peer influences, drugs, alcohol, abusive relationships, sexual pitfalls, or other negative experiences, intervene quickly, because just like an overtime, shootout, or extra-inning game, life can forever be altered or changed suddenly.

No doubt you have found or will find yourself putting "overtime" into many of your student-athletes who need special attention, advice, or spiritual guidance. Cherish and thank God for those overtime and extra-special moments when you can be a caring Christian leader and make an everlasting impression and impact on young people who look up to and admire you so much.

While overtimes, shootouts, and extra-inning games raise the stakes and create a more nerve-wracking sporting experience, not knowing Jesus Christ or God's Word is much more frightening. Just as you do not wait to coach your best or hope your athletes save their best in reserve for overtimes, shootouts, and extra innings that may not ever come to fruition, do not save or wait to share the best and most meaningful coaching lessons and faith applications for some practice or moment down the road. Jesus preached and delivered on His mission right up until He triumphantly stated on the cross, "It is finished" (John 19:30).

Like any overtime, shootout, or extra-inning game, the time you have with your student-athletes will come to an end sooner and more suddenly than you think, so share God's Word and Jesus with your team today. Put some overtime and extra thought into how you can use your platform to teach your athletes that they have nothing to fear in life with Jesus by their side. Not even sudden death.

A DEVOTION FROM THE COACH TO THE ATHLETES

You also must be ready, for the Son of Man is coming at an hour you do not expect. (Luke 12:40)

Heaven and earth will pass away, but My words will not pass away. (Matthew 24:35)

As much as I would rather win in regulation time, I know that we will sometimes find ourselves in intense overtimes/shootouts/extra-inning games. When those moments come, I hope you remember what got you there: the fundamentals, training, drills, teamwork, and systems we have employed and worked on throughout the entire season.

One wonderful aspect is that even if you have played poorly throughout regulation, overtimes and extra innings give you an opportunity for redemption. If you controlled the ball poorly throughout the game, you still can help your team by scoring in the shootout. If you struck out four times, you can get the key two-out hit to drive the winning run home.

Just like it is never too late to get a game winning goal or hit, it is never too late in life to know Jesus as your Lord and Savior. I hope you remember this when it comes to your friends and loved ones who might not know Jesus. Do not wait till the very end of your life or theirs to share Jesus or God's Word with them. You never know when that last day might be.

Another cool thing about overtimes/shootouts/extra-inning games, particularly if you win, is you get to compete in the sport you love for a little while longer. The hard part, especially if you lose, is that the end comes abruptly. There is no chance to keep playing and make up a deficit or come back. The game, the tournament, the season—any of them can be all over in the blink of an eye. That's why they often call extra-inning games, overtime periods, and shootouts sudden-death moments.

You know what is more tragic than losing in overtime or extra-innings, or even knowing that this could be your last day on earth? More scary than those is living and dying without knowing Jesus Christ as your personal Lord and Savior.

That is why we do team devotions. I want you to know and hear, again and again, that your relationship with Jesus is way more important than playing the sport you love. This is why we encourage one another to go to church, where we hear God's Word, confess our sins, and receive God's forgiveness. This is why we read the Bible and let the Holy Spirit work on strengthening our faith. This is why we celebrate and give thanks for what Jesus did for us on the cross.

Thinking of how overtimes/shootouts/extra-inning games come to an end so suddenly, I do not want this season to go by and end without you knowing how much I care about you. And if I truly care about you, then I need to remind you how much Jesus loves you. As fired up as I get coaching you on the finer aspects of our team and sport, your relationship with Jesus is what really matters in life. Thanks to Him, you and I do not even have to fear sudden death, because we will live forever with Him someday in heaven.

So let's win our contests before they get to overtime! Okay? More important, remember that Jesus will always be with you no matter what you face in life and when you face it.

A PRAYER FOR THE ATHLETES

Dear heavenly Father,

We know that while there is sin and death, even sudden death, in this fallen world, Jesus defeated sin, death, and the power of the devil once and for all when He died on the cross and rose again. Since we do not know when our earthly days will be over, inspire us to cherish each day and live it to the fullest as we cling to the cross and empty tomb at all times.

In the name of the Father, the Son, and the Holy Spirit. Amen.

A Big-Time Banquet

"And bring the fattened calf and kill it, and let us eat and celebrate. For this my son was dead, and is alive again; he was lost, and is found." And they began to celebrate.
(Luke 15:23–24)

Also that everyone should eat and drink and take pleasure in all his toil—this is God's gift to man.
(Ecclesiastes 3:13)

FOR THE COACH

Christian leaders should be the kings and queens of closure and celebration. Jesus, who rose triumphantly on Easter Sunday after enduring a horrific crucifixion on Good Friday, is our Savior as well as our inspiration for celebrating. He paid the price for our sins and won for us our salvation. Someday in the not too distant future, His followers will be called home and join Him in paradise—a place where streets are paved with gold and, most important, where we will see and be with Jesus in all His glory. Death on earth is not our end but the beginning of eternity in heaven. What a blessed finish awaits all who know Jesus as Lord and Savior! Among other things, our heavenly homecoming will be one eternal party and celebration with the saints and the Lamb of God.

No matter how many wins and losses your team had, no matter if your team performed below expectations or exceeded them, you have the responsibility and opportunity to close your season with class. You can rejoice with your players and their families, celebrate the season and the most important thing (MIT) in life. So, before you pack up the uniforms and lock up the equipment, go big and go bold with some kind of formal banquet or end of the season celebration. Make the closure event your masterpiece that differentiates and accentuates your program and coaching philosophy.

There are many things you can do to make your end-of-season banquet big-time and meaningful. Certainly, you reflect on the season and present off-season expectations for the future of the program, but do not stop there. Get personal about your student-athletes. Take the time to really reflect on what you want to say about each of them because most of your athletes will never forget your words. Saying substantive and meaningful things about your athletes in front of their family, friends, and peers is a big deal and certainly leaves a legacy.

On the night of the banquet or celebration, invite each athlete to come up front. Share a story or meaningful moment about each individual. Celebrate each one's gifts in athletics but also life beyond the sport. Let the laughter, tears, and specific praise flow in a way that reveals and demonstrates your respect and love for the individuals on your team. This is your last chance to make a lasting impression on these young student-athletes. Very few people ever have anything special or significant stated about them publicly. You will be surprised how much your student-athletes remember about your body language, disposition, tone, and, of course, the words you speak about them. Cherish this special opportunity.

The truth is that you demanded a lot from these athletes over the past months. Perhaps you were too hard on some and not as loving as you could have been toward others. Perhaps you do not have much to say about the individuals who did not see much playing time or did not compete as much as others in terms of athletic play. Remember, however, that these are the kids, as well as their moms and dads, who especially need and want to hear that you recognized their specialness beyond their athletic prowess and abilities (or lack thereof).

Embrace the one final chance God has given you to make an impact on their lives. Tell the audience why each team member is special and a blessing from God. Share what you love about each kid and how they were, and are, a blessing in your life. Inspire and shape these student-athletes with affirmation and encouragement.

You have a prominent platform to share the faith and remind everyone about the MIT in a very personal way during your season-ending banquet. At this point in the season, your secular scorecard is already complete. There are no more games, matches, meets, or competitions. Your athletes' spiritual scorecards, however, are still undergoing construction and growth. They are still running the race to receive the prize (1 Corinthians 9:24).

Share God's Word one last time with your athletes and their families. Make some faith connections in regard to their individual contributions to the team. Celebrate and recognize each kid as a special child of God. Bring the joy of Jesus to your celebration, and leave a Christ-centered legacy. Be the Christian Coach of the Year *and* the Christian coach of their lifetime.

A DEVOTION FROM THE COACH TO THE ATHLETES

I thank my God in all my remembrance of you. (Philippians 1:3)

And those twelve stones, which they took out of the Jordan, Joshua set up at Gilgal. And he said to the people of Israel, "When your children ask their fathers in times to come, 'What do these stones mean?' then you shall let your children know, 'Israel passed over this Jordan on dry ground.' For the Lord your God dried up the waters of the Jordan for you until you passed over, as the Lord your God did to the Red Sea, which He dried up for us until we passed over, so that all the peoples of the earth may know that the hand of the Lord is mighty, that you may fear the Lord your God forever." (Joshua 4:20–24)

Joshua set up stones so that the children of Israel would remember what God had done for them. I hope all of you have some stones, or special memories, that you will always remember from this past season.

The Bible tells us there is a time for everything (Ecclesiastes 3). Tonight is the time to reflect upon a completed season and to celebrate the many blessings God bestowed upon us individually and collectively as a team/program. There are many different emotions that come with the end of something. Some of us are relieved and ready to move on to something different. Others might be saddened or feel a sense of loss that the season is over.

Whatever your emotions tonight, I want you to know that you are all special individuals, and I am so grateful to God for placing each of you in my life.

I thank God for bringing this team together and for the opportunity to compete in our sport. Millions of kids across the globe—because of poverty, hunger, political upheaval, family tragedy, war, and other challenges—will never have the same opportunity that we did. Moreover, I give thanks for the cherished relationships formed and friendships enriched over the course of this season, for the successful and fun times and, yes, even for the trials, challenges, and tough times we experienced. For "we know that for those who love God all things work together for good, for those who are called according to His purpose" (Romans 8:28).

As much as we may love our sport, we know that it is just a sport. Many other things are much more important in life, primarily our relationship with God. Whether we win or lose, God still loves us. Scripture says that each of you remains the apple of His eye.

So, tonight, let us give thanks to God—the Alpha and Omega, the beginning and the end—from whom all blessings flow.

A FINAL PRAYER FOR THE ATHLETES

Dear heavenly Father,

Thank you for sending Your Son, Jesus, to take away our sins so that we might one day join You for eternity in heaven. We are victorious in life only because of what Jesus did for us on that cross. Our competitive sports days will end sometime in the future, but not Your love for us. May we always celebrate Your victory over sin, death, and the power of the devil. To You be all praise, honor, and glory, forever and ever.

In the name of the Father, the Son, and the Holy Spirit. Amen.

The Can-Do List

There are literally hundreds of things you can do as a coach or leader to share and teach the faith to your athletes during the season. Below is a Can-Do List which may or may not be applicable to your specific coaching context (factoring in things such as age, skill level, competition, etc.). The list is not exhaustive but meant to inspire you to consider the many different ways and opportunities God provides for you in your coaching platform. Coach 'em up!

Pick a Bible Verse or Biblical Theme for the Season

You know your athletes better than anyone. Pick a Bible verse that resonates with your team members—their personalities, challenges, strengths, peculiarities, special opportunities, and so on. If you pick the theme or verse, you will be more prone to stick with it throughout the season. Display it on T-shirts, scouting reports, player posters, PowerPoints, program handbooks, and handouts at your parent meetings. Put the verse or theme in your digital calendar every Monday so that you are reminded to reflect on and refocus on the theme too.

Require Your Athletes to Give One Devotion

If student-athletes hear something, they *might* remember it. If they see something in action, they *probably* will remember it. If they have to teach something, they *assuredly* will remember it, so have each one of your athletes give a devotion throughout the season on your team's Bible verse or theme or on something fresh from their own perspective. The devotion does not have to be long. Let their creativity reign. Put your captains in charge to see that each student-athlete participates and does a quality job. Collect these devotions and assemble them in the end-of-the-year keepsake or scrapbook you plan to give to your athletes.

Make and Give a Scrapbook or Keepsake of Your Season

No matter how artistic you are (or not), put together a scrapbook to give to your student-athletes at the end of the season. Get a parent or support staff person to help you make it look good if you want, but the important feature is to make it personal. Write down ten things you will always remember about each athlete. Be uplifting and affirming. Compliment them on their God-given athletic gifts if you want but especially on the dispositions and attributes that have more to do with their uniqueness and identity in Christ. Tell them why God made them special. Include humorous stories or moments from the season if you wish, but make sure your account does not embarrass them. In addition, share a favorite Bible verse, devotional thought, or personal prayer for each player in their profile. They might not ever receive a yearbook or scrapbook as meaningful as this one. Look for it to be proudly displayed at their graduation parties someday.

Make Your Prayers Specific and Special

Many Christian teams pray together. You, however, can make your team prayers more sticky in your athletes' minds by connecting them to something sport specific or personal. For example, if a lot of conditioning drills are on the practice schedule, you could focus your prayer on staying in good shape spiritually by reading God's Word or regular church attendance. The point is to be intentional in helping your athletes think and reflect on their relationship with God.

Post Some Pics with Some Bible Scripts

Kids love social media and looking at pictures. So why not make it a personal goal to post at least one "behind-the-scenes" picture, or action shot, of each team member on social media throughout the course of the season. Attach a Bible verse to the picture and write why or how the particular verse reminds you of each individual on your team. Your athletes will always remember the verse you selected and what you wrote about them. A picture and a special Bible verse are worth way more than a thousand words.

Set Faith Goals

Often teams, athletes, and coaches set goals. As you help organize the goal-setting for your team, encourage each athlete to set at least one goal that relates to their Christian faith walk. Whether it be reading at least one Bible verse a day, spending more time in prayer, leading the team in a devotion, organizing a volunteer activity, or finding different ways to encourage teammates, let your student-athletes set their own faith goals. Have them assess themselves on their goal each month and turn it in to you with a rationale. Set at least one faith goal for yourself too.

Initiate Operation Warm-Fuzzy Friday

Every Friday, take it upon yourself to write an uplifting and encouraging note to at least two of your athletes, their parents, or other supporters associated with the program. Tell them how blessed you are to have them in your life. Nurture the faith by including a special Bible verse for whatever occasion you have to write them the note. Let them marinate all weekend in your faith-filled communication and edifying words. If nothing else goes well on Friday, at least you will have filled two people's spiritual buckets with encouragement and God's Word.

Create a Hall (or Halls) of Faith

School classroom walls are filled with pictures, posters, white-boards, technology, and all kinds of educational communication. So why not fill your locker room walls with Bible verses, pictures of biblical heroes, motivational posters, articles depicting athletes giving a Christian testimony, or sports action shots accompanied by Scripture passages? There is an old saying that "if only these walls could talk." They can. Perhaps you can even make them sing. Surround your athletes with God's Word and inspiration. Ask them to contribute to and use their creativity and artistry on the Halls of Faith too.

Solicit Faith Feedback from Parents

Remember during your parent meeting when you told every-one that God comes first, then family, then schoolwork, and then your sport? Consider soliciting feedback from parents during the season. Email or send hard copies home of your athletes' person-al and team goals, and ask parents to give you feedback on how their child is doing on their goals, including the faith ones. Send out a first-, second-, third-, and fourth-quarter feedback request. This process not only gives you good insight as to what is being discussed at the kitchen table, but it also shows parents your com-mitment to their child's faith growth and walk. Moreover, it keeps the lines of communication open with parents. Finally, you and your athletes just might give a terrific Christian testimonial to some parents who might not be as solid in their relationship with Jesus as their child may be.

Go Viral with Christ's Victory

Use a digital diary, blog, Facebook link, or Twitter feed (with seasonal hashtag) to post spiritual reflections you have about your team. Elaborate on devotional discussions your team had or anything that comes to mind in regard to a faith moment you all experienced. Truly take the time to reflect on God's benevolence and how He continues to bless you and your team in so many ways. Allow your athletes to post on your Dear Basketball Diary or Dear Volleyball Diary platform too. By focusing on the faith scorecard rather than secular scorecard, this diary or blog can be a safe place where all of your athletes are affirmed and uplifted while, at the same time, providing a good testimony of the faith.

Schedule a Few Team Service Projects

You do not want to overschedule these events and take student-athletes away from their families more than your sport and practice schedule already does, but team service projects can be a wonderful way to live and share the faith. Whether volunteering at a Special Olympics event, soup kitchen, or youth sports camp, get your student-athletes involved in helping others. Whatever you decide to do, make sure you make the point to your athletes that we serve and show love to others because Christ first served and loved us all the way to the cross.

Establish a Christian Athlete Reader Club

Anytime you find an uplifting Christian testimony about an athlete in a newspaper, blog, YouTube clip, or elsewhere, share it with your team. Build a file throughout the year so that you can share them during the season. Send the articles, videos, or stories on the weekend when your athletes may have more time to read or view them. Ask them to comment on the article or video, either online or in your team meeting. Christian readers become Christian leaders.

Go to Church Together as a Team

You want to be careful not to take your student-athletes away from their families or home congregation too much, but attending the worship service together as a team is always something memorable and special. Moreover, this may be the only time some of your athletes ever get to church. If Sunday mornings do not work logistically, make an effort to attend an Advent or Lenten service together after practice. Eat dinner as a team before or after the service. Keep building those relationships with one another, and let the Holy Spirit continue to work on the hearts and minds of you and your team members.

Take Advantage of Special Opportunities

Be on the lookout for opportunities that engage your student-athletes in their faith walk and growth. Is there a new movie or YouTube video just out that portrays the challenges of living as a Christian or being a Christian athlete? See it together as a team and talk about it. Does some civic organization, such as the local Rotary Club or Chamber of Commerce, want your athletes to come and talk to their group? Show up and give a Christian testimony. Share the faith when a newspaper or blog writer asks to do a story on one of your athletes or team.

Grow in Your Own Faith and Christian Servant Leadership

Of all the things you can do for your athletes' faith walk, none is more important than *you* growing in your relationship with Jesus. Be in church regularly and faithfully. Pray for your athletes that the Holy Spirit would work in their lives too. Get in the Word and stay in the Word. Receive God's grace and the Holy Spirit so that your faith can be renewed and strengthened. You cannot fake faithfulness, at least not in God's eyes. To be the Christian leader the young people need you to be, you must be a faithful follower of Christ. By yourself, you cannot do anything. With Jesus, all things are possible.